LEARNERS WITH ATTENTION DEFICIT HYPERACTIVITY DISORDER

LEARNERS WITH ATTENTION DEFICIT HYPERACTIVITY DISORDER

By

Dr. Rashmi Choudhuri

Associate Professor

Banaras Hindu University

Varanasi (U.P.)

(India)

DPH

DISCOVERY PUBLISHING HOUSE PVT. LTD.

NEW DELHI-110 002

Published by:
Tilak Wasan
DISCOVERY PUBLISHING HOUSE PVT. LTD.
4383/4A, Ansari Road, Darya Ganj
New Delhi-110 002 (India)
Phone : +91-11-23279245, 43596064-65
Fax : +91-11-23253475
E-mail : parul.wasan@gmail.com
discoverypublishinghouse@gmail.com
web : www.discoverypublishinggroup.com

First Edition: **2012**
ISBN: 978-93-5056-104-1

Learners with Attention Deficit Hyperactivity Disorder

Printed at:
Shree Balaji Art Press
Delhi

Preface

Teaching is an exciting and challenging job, more so when one ventures into a field of study that is relatively new. Developmental disorder particularly attention deficit hyperactivity disorder is an upcoming field which has lately drawn and engaged attention of the researchers in special education. In recent years much has been documented about it in journals of education, psychology and psychiatry which could be incorporated in books on special education.

This book was prompted by an enchantment with the investigations made about it and the perception of the need for a text to describe the what is and the what can be.

Attention deficit hyperactivity disorder results in children and adolescents exhibiting inappropriate behaviour and being unable to learn as spontaneously or quickly as the other typical children. Children and adolescents with this disorder are likely to be misunderstood in the school and community because of their behaviours which they are unable to control. Teachers have difficult time dealing with them, particularly when they are ignorant about the disorder and the necessary interventions.

The primary objective is to present the text in a way that would be helpful to the prospective teachers, students of education, students of special education and researchers.

The research studies have been included to allow for a clear cut perspective. This text is intended to bridge the initial and recent knowledge on the subject by reviewing research literature.

The text is organized into five chapters. Chapter 1 reflects what is known and understood about attention deficit hyperactivity disorder. Chapter 2 contains characteristics. Chapter 3 deals with etiology of the disorder. Chapter 4 outlines the identification and assessment, and chapter 5 relates to the interventions, education and teacher preparation.

I hope that a sense of excitement and mastery have been communicated and that the text encourages a sense of learning beyond a mere text. The entire approach is intended to be positive and challenging.

Author

Acknowledgement

In the preparation of this book many studies of scholars published in various books and journals have been consulted. I am indebted to the distinguished scholars whose studies contribute to the book's content. Their contribution has been acknowledged in the form of reference at the end of the text.

I sincerely appreciate the encouragement and guidance given by my teachers and colleagues from time to time. Most of all, I owe my loving thanks to my friend Dr. Archana Singh who has been a constant source of motivation and inspiration and helped me get through this difficult task of writing a book.

I cannot forget the contribution of my students who in more ways than one have taught me about the subject.

Finally, my parents have been a source of encouragement and immense help. The actual writing required their patience and understanding.

The typing of this text also required significant effort. I owe my thanks to Mr. Sonu who painstakingly undertook the task of typing the text.

Contents

CHAPTER 1

Conceptualization about ADHD

Introduction

Attention deficit hyperactivity disorder (ADHD) is the most updated label used for a disorder with characteristic behaviour pattern of overactivity, impulsivity, and/or inattention. These set of behaviours are displayed at developmentally inappropriate levels. The difficulties posed by ADHD are mostly persistent which interfere with many areas of typical development and functioning in a child's life. It is a childhood problem which often continues into adolescence and adulthood. It is one of the most commonly diagnosed disorders of childhood and is also the most extensively studied problem of childhood.

Complexities and debate surround the etiology, diagnosis and management of ADHD. Some researchers maintain that it should be considered as more than just a neurobiological/ developmental disorder (Akram et al., 2009). Some regard it as a psychiatric disorder of childhood (e.g. Barkley, 1997a).

The essential behaviours characterizing ADHD, i.e., hyperactivity, impulsivity and/or inattention appear early in a child's life in the preschool and early school years (Bauermeister et al., 1995; Barkley, 1997b, 1997c). Since, these symptoms may be seen in many typically developing children but at a low level, or the symptoms may be due to some other disorder, it is important that a thorough examination and appropriate diagnosis is done by a well qualified professional.

Characteristics of ADHD appear over the course of many months, often impulsiveness and hyperactivity appearing before inattention, which may emerge after a year or still later. Characteristic behaviours that appear may be different depending upon the type of ADHD. They may also be different in different types of settings, depending upon the demands of the situation posed on the child for self control (Kendall, 2000). A child who does not sit still will be noticeable in school but not in play situation. On the other hand, the inattentive, day dreaming child may not be noticed in school. The impulsive child who acts without thinking may be considered just as an indisciplined child, while the child who is passive or sluggish may be viewed as merely unmotivated (Kendall, 2000). Yet they may have different types of ADHD. Restlessness, acting without thinking, and daydreaming are sometimes seen in all children. It is when the characteristics of hyperactivity, distractibility, poor concentration, or impulsivity in a child begin to affect performance in school, social relationships with other children, or behaviour at home, that ADHD may be suspected. The essential characteristic features need to be displayed across multiple settings before ADHD is confirmed. However, it is not easy to diagnose ADHD since the characteristics vary too much across situations. This is especially true when the primary characteristic is inattentiveness.

Historical Background

ADHD was first described by Dr. Heinrich Hoffman in 1845. He was a physician who wrote books on medicine and psychiatry and was also a poet. He wrote a book of poems about children and their characteristics. He accurately described a little boy who had attention deficit hyperactivity disorder in 'The story of fidgety Philip'. But it was later in 1902, that Sir George F. Still made recognition of ADHD easier. He published a series of lectures to the Royal College of Physicians in England in which he described a group of impulsive children with distinguishable attribute of inappropriate social conduct and significant behavioural problems, or children with ADHD as recognized today.

Historically the conceptualization of attention deficit hyperactivity disorder and its terminology have been subjected to several revisions after it was first recognized as a typical disorder. The terms used for it have been minimal brain dysfunction, hyperkinetic reaction and attention deficit disorder. Its symptoms have been redefined, reorganized and renamed a number of times in the past. In the early 1920s some researchers (eg. Strecker & Ebaugh, 1924) drew attention to a group of children who had survived the encephalitis outbreak in 1917-18 in North America (Lowe & Reynolds, 2000). They described about inattentiveness, impulsiveness and socially disruptive behaviour in this group of children who were left with the disorder as a result of brain damage.

In 1940s and 1950s there was a rise in reserach on the disorder. Children's problems of inattentiveness, impulsiveness, restlessness, overactivity, and distractibility were described (e.g. Strauss & Lehtinen, 1947) and attributed to brain damage. So during this period a new term was given to describe these children whose major problem was their excessively high activity (Lowe & Reynolds, 2000). This new term for the disorder was Minimal Brain Damage (MBD).

In the next decade that is in the 1960s reserches undertaken could not produce evidence to link exessively high activity to brain damage. So, the label Minimal Brain Damage was dropped and replaced by another term, Minimal Brain Dysfunction.

Thereafter, in the following decades particularly during the three decades from late 1960s to 1990s, conceptualization of ADHD changed repeatedly in the two widely known classification systems—North American psychiatric diagnostic classification system, known as Diagnostic and Statistical Manual of Mental Disorders (American Psychological Association) and International Classification of Diseases developed by the World Health Organization (WHO). The revisions done in the two classification systems are presented here, one by one.

Revisions in Diagnostic and Statistical Manual of Mental Disorders (DSM)

In 1968, the term used to describe attention deficit hyperactivity disorder was hyperkinetic reaction of childhood, in place of the term Minimal Brain Dysfunction. This term was first mentioned in the second edition of the *Diagnostic and Statistical Manual of Mental Disorders* (DSM-II, American Psychiatric Association, 1968). At the time excessive motor activity was the essential feature of the disorder and this term reflected that view.

In 1980, when the third edition of DSM was published (DSM-III, American Psychiatric Association, 1980) inattentive behaviour became the central feature of the disorder. ADHD comprised of three dimensions : inattention, impulsivity and hyperactivity. These dimensions were manifested in two distinct diagnostic categories or subtypes : (*i*) Attention Deficit Disorder (ADD) that occurred with Hyperactivity (ADD/H) and (*ii*) Attention Deficit Disorder (ADD) that occurred without Hyperactivity (ADD/WO) (American Psychiatric Association, 1980). Thus, the children who exhibited both inattention and hyperactivity were given the term Attention Deficit Disorder with Hyperactivity (ADD/H). On the other hand, children who displayed only attention problems were designated as Attention Deficit Disorder without Hyperactivity (ADD/WO).

Later on, a number of factor analysis studies were done to explore, identify and confirm the separate variables or factors underlying ADHD. Factor analyses done in the studies consistently indicated that symptoms of ADHD are best described by separate dimensions composed of symptoms of hyperactivity impulsivity and symptoms of inattention (Bauermeister, 1992; Burns, Walsh, Owen, & Snell, 1997; Conners, Sitarenios, Parker, & Epstein, 1998a, 1998b; DuPaul et al., 1997; DuPaul et al., 1998a; Healy et al., 1993; cited in Willcutt & Pennington, 2000, p.180)

By 1987, in the revised edition of DSM-III (American Psychiatric Association, 1987) distinction between the two subtypes was dropped and all the three symptoms of inattention, hyperactivity and impulsivity were integrated and merged into a single diagnostic category of Attention-Deficit Hyperactivity Disorder (ADHD). The diagnosis of ADD/WO was dropped in this edition. A residual category Undifferentiated Attention Deficit Disorder (UADD), was included in this revised edition of DSM-III (DSM-III-R) for children who exhibit pure inattentive behaviour. However, list of symptoms for this category were not included (Lahey et al., 1988).

The fourth edition of the DSM (DSM-IV, American Psychiatric Association, 1994) differentiates three subtypes within a broad diagnostic category of ADHD replacing the previous single diagnostic category. The three subtypes are : a predominantly inattentive type (ADHD-I), a predominantly hyperactivity impulsivity type (ADHD-HI), and a combined type (ADHD-C). This categorization of ADHD is maintained in later revision of DSM-IV TR (DSM-IV Text Revised).

So the formal designation of the disorder, as of now, is Attention-Deficit Hyperactivity Disorder (ADHD), with three subtypes in it-ADHD-I, ADHD-HI and ADHD-C. Children are diagnosed with ADHD only if symptoms are frequently exhibited for at least six months, and are present prior to age seven according to DSM-IV criteria.

Revisions in International Classification of Diseases (ICD)

The first term given for ADHD by the International Classification of Disease-9 (ICD-9) was hyperkinetic syndrome of childhood (WHO, 1977). This term was used to describe a disorder of the childhood, the essential features of which were short attention spam, distractibility and overactivity (WHO, 1978). Later the term was changed to hyperkinetic disorders in the next publication of ICD, i.e. ICD-10 (WHO 1992a, 1992b). The symptoms for diagnosing hyperkinetic disorders in the ICD-10 (Diagnostic criteria for Research; DCR-10; WHO, 1993) are almost identical to the ADHD symptoms mentioned in the DSM-IV. However some differences are seen in the two classification systems. DCR-10 requires at least 10 out of 18 symptoms for diagnosis whereas DSM-IV require at least 6 symptoms in one area. Also, one of the items 'often talk excessively' is considered to be a symptom of impulsivity in the DCR-10, but in the DSM-IV it is considered to be a hyperactive symptom (Yang, Schaller & Parker, 2000).

DIAGNOSTIC CHARACTERISTICS

Inattention

Children who are inattentive seem not to listen, shift rapidly from one activity to another before completing the first one, which shows short attention span (Alessandri, 1992), and may get bored with a task after only a few minutes. They go from one toy to another without focussed play with either toy; in the classroom they are easily distracted and fail to pay attention to directions.

If they are doing something they really enjoy, they do not have difficulty in paying attention (Kendall, 2000). But focussing deliberate, conscious attention to organizing and completing a task or learning something new is difficult for them.

Doing homework is particularly hard for these children. They tend to forget writing down an assignment, or forget to bring a book, or bring the wrong book. The homework, if finally completed, is full of mistakes and erasures. Completing homework is often frustrating for both parent and child.

The DSM-IV-TR gives these signs of inattention (at least six of the following are needed for diagnosis).

- Often getting distracted easily by irrelevant sights and sounds.
- Often failing to pay close attention to details and making careless mistakes in school, work or other activities.
- Often having difficulty in sustaining attention in talks or play activities.
- Often not seeming to listen to what is being said to him or her.
- Often not careful in following instructions, and often failing to complete schoolwork or other tasks.
- Often losing or forgetting things and tools needed for a task like toys, pencils, or books.
- Often forgetting matters in day-to-day activities.
- Often having difficulty in organizing any task or activity, or often skipping from one unfinished task to another.
- Often avoiding or disliking tasks that require sustained mental effort.

The exact nature of attentional problems seen in ADHD children is being studied; whether the problem is tied to inability to pay attention or to difficulty in sustaining attention is being researched and much progress has been made.

Hyperactivity

Children who are hyperactive show excessive levels of motor activity. Such children are restless and seem to be constantly in motion. They are always dashing around touching objects or playing with whatever is in sight or talk incessantly. They are unable to play quietly. They may try to do several things at a time. Sitting still is hard for them even while taking their meals or during a lesson in classroom. They are fidgety, squirm in their seats, or often leave their seats. Or else they may wiggle their feet or tap their pencil. These children are so overactive doing something or the other that parents and teachers cannot keep up with them. They are also inept at shifting from unstructured, free activities to structured activities such as from school recess to a classroom activity (Kendall, 2000).

Signs of hyperactivity given in DSM-IV-TR are :

- Feeling restless, often fidgeting with hands or feet, or squirming while seated.
- Often running, climbing excessively in situations when it is inappropriate.
- Often leaving a seat or talking excessively in situations where sitting or quiet behaviour is expected.
- Often having difficulty playing or engaging in leisure activities.

Impulsivity

Impulsive children generally do not think before they act and seem unable to stop their immediate reactions. Although typically developing children in general, can be impulsive (especially at younger ages), children with ADHD are more prone to be impulsive. They routinely blurt out answers to questions or inappropriate comments and often interrupt others. They are impaired in the ability to inhibit inappropriate responses (Jennings *et al.*, 1997). They display their emotions without restraint, and act without regard for the later consequences of their conduct. They fail to wait for their turn due to impulsivity. Thus it is hard for them to be patient till their turn comes whether in games, class or for any other matter. They may grab a toy from another child or hit when they are upset. They have problems organizing schoolwork and generally need much closer supervision. Even as teenagers or adults, they may impulsively choose to do things that have an immediate but small payoff rather than engage in activities which provide much greater but delayed rewards. The problem of impulsivity can be understood with examples in different contexts. In the ground while playing football, the impulsive child runs onto the field chasing the ball, not yet knowing the team he was on or which goal to shoot toward (Kendall, 2000). In the classroom, the impulsive child starts giving answer before listening to the complete question, or even before the teacher asks him to answer the question.

Signs of impulsivity given in DSM-IV-TR are :

- Often blurting out answers before hearing the whole question.
- Often having difficulty in waiting or taking turns.
- Often interrupting or intruding on others.

At least six signs of hyperactivity / Impulsivity mentioned need to be seen for diagnosis.

Limitations of DSM-IV Criteria

The items based on DSM-IV criteria may not be appropriate for all ages and may fail to adequately sample instances of attention, hyperactivity-impulsivity, and executive dysfunction over the entire span of life (Wolf, 2001). Since symptoms of hyperactivity and impulsivity are prominent at the younger ages, more common symptoms of childhood may be overrepresented in the DSM-IV criteria (Barkley, 2006). This requires adults to present with more severe symptoms in order to be diagnosed. In addition, ADHD symptoms may manifest somewhat differently in adulthood than in childhood. For example, symptoms of internal restlessness may be displayed more likely by adults with ADHD, whereas the core ADHD symptoms of inattention, hyperactivity, and impulsivity are overt in children. Thus to identify ADHD in adults, internal restlessness may be a salient quality to be sampled. Also, attention is treated as a single, undifferentiated entity in the DSM-IV diagnosis of ADHD, despite the existence of several separate attention systems (see attention in chapter 2). The DSM-IV symptoms used to diagnose ADHD do not categorize individuals with ADHD into subgroups according to the different attention system possessed by them. The conventional approach of lumping all children with ADHD into one attentional category seems clearly unwarranted (Tsal, Shalev & Mevorach, 2005, p. 154).

Classification

Diagnostic and statistical manual for Mental Disorders (DSM-IV TR) provides different patterns of behaviour for different types of ADHD. Individuals with ADHD may exhibit signs of consistent inattentiveness. They may exhibit a pattern of hyperactive-impulsive behaviour far exceeding that of others of the same age. Or they may show hyperactive-impulsive behaviour alongwith inattentiveness. Elevatedly exhibited signs on either dimension is sufficient to warrant a diagnosis of ADHD, with elevations on both dimensions indicating the presence of a combined type of ADHD. Thus three subtypes of ADHD are recognized by professionals. These are :

1. Predominantly inattentive type (that does not show significant hyperactive impulsive behaviour) sometimes called ADD-an outdated term for this entire disorder;
2. Predominantly hyperactive impulsive type (that does not show significant inattention); and
3. Combined type (that exhibits both inattentive and hyperactive impulsive behaviour).

These conditions somewhat differ in description but further research is required for the possibility that these separate disorders.

(1) Predominantly inattentive type of ADHD: Children with the predominantly inattentive type of ADHD are rarely impulsive or hyperactive, but they have significant problems paying attention. They appear to be day dreaming, sluggish, underactive, shy and easily confused. They exhibit difficulties with perceptual motor speed and processing (Barkley et al., 1992). They may have difficulty processing information as quickly and accurately as other children. When the teacher gives oral or written instructions, they may not grasp it. They have a hard time understanding what they are supposed to do and make frequent mistakes. However they may sit quietly, and even appear to be working but not fully attending to or understanding the task and the instructions. They end up making frequent mistakes.

These children do not show significant problems with impulsivity and hyperactivity in classroom, on the school ground or at home. They may get along better with other children than more impulsive, and hyperactive and combined types of ADHD children.

(2) Predominantly hyperactive impulsive type of ADHD: Children with predominantly hyperactive and impulsive type of ADHD do not show significant inattention. These children are more likely to have impaired performance on tasks requiring behavioural inhibition (Barkley et al., 1992). They are viewed negatively by their peers because of their rule violations, non compliance and aggression. The social rejection experienced by children with this type of ADHD appears to develop after only brief periods of interaction with others (Bickett & Milich 1990, cited in Kendall, 2000). This subtype is relatively rare and generally occurs only in younger typically preschool age children (Elia, Ambrosini, & Berrettini, 2008; Lahey et al., 1994). In fact, recent research suggests that ADHD-hyperactive-impulsive may not represent a distinct subtype but rather an early diagnosis of ADHD that later develops into ADHD-combined (Lahey, Pelham, Loney, Lee & Willcutt, 2005; Riley et al., 2008). Even earlier literature suggested that hyperactivity symptoms decrease with age (eg. Barkley, 1998a; Heiligenstein et al., 1998b; Hill & Schroener, 1996).

(3) Combined type of ADHD: Children with combined type of ADHD exhibit both inattentiveness and impulsive hyperactive behaviour in significant manner.

Co-existence of ADHD with other Disorders and Difficulties

ADHD, quite commonly, exists with other difficulties and disorders. ADHD children are at risk for developing comorbid disorders. At least one more disorder is found in approximately 44 per cent (Szatsmari, Offord & Boyle, 1989) to 50 per cent (Barkley, 1998b, cited in Lowe & Reynolds, 2000) of children with ADHD. Some of them have more than one comorbid disorder.

The disorders co-occurring with ADHD are: (1) Learning disability; (2) Socio-emotional and behavioural impairment/ psychiatric disorders; (3) Social impairments. Some children with ADHD have more than one comorbid disorder.

(1) Learning disability : 20 to 30 per cent of ADHD children have co-existing specific learning disabilities (Wender, 2002). In preschool years these disabilities include difficulty in understanding certain sounds or words and/or difficulty in expressing oneself in words. The school age children have learning disabilities in mathematics, reading (Reid *et al.*, 1994, & Barkley, 1998b; Gross-Tsur, Manor, & Shalev, 1996), spelling (MTA Cooperative Group, 1999) and handwriting (Barkley, 1998b). The co-occurrence of ADHD and learning disailities in youth have also been reported (e.g. Semrud-Clikeman et al., 1992; Shaywitz et al., 1995).

Estimates of the prevalence of learning disability alongwith ADHD range from 15 per cent to 50 per cent for reading (August & Garfinkel, 1990; Barkley, 1990; Mayes, Calhoun & Crowell, 2000; Semrud-Clikeman, et al., 1992) from 24 per cent to 60 per cent for arithmetic (Barkley, 1990; Semrud-Clikeman et al., 1992) from 24 per cent to 60 per cent for spelling (Barkley, 1990; Mayes, Calhoun & Crowell, 2000) and 65.1 per cent for written expression (Mayes, Calhoun, & Crowell, 2000). Many children with ADHD have learning disability in more than one area.

ADHD and learning disabilities are independently transmitted in families and are etiologically distinct. Independent transmission of ADHD and dyscalculia (Monuteaux, Faraone, Herzig et al., 2005), ADHD and reading disability (Gilger, Penington, & DeFries, 1992), and, ADHD and spelling disability (Stevenson, Pennington, Gilger, DeFries, & Gillis, 1993) have been shown in research studies.

(2) Socio-emotional and behavioural impairment/ psychiatric disorders : Children and youth with ADHD are also at increased risk for concomitant externalizing and internalizing disorders. Many children with ADHD demonstrate high rates of aggressive and other externalizing behaviour problems (Treuting & Hinshaw, 2001). The most common externalizing behavioural disorders co-ocurring with ADHD are conduct disorder and oppositional defiant disorder (ODD) (Lowe & Reynolds, 2000; Lahey, McBurnett, & Loeber, 2000; Jensen et al., 2001).

ADHD children and adolescents with conduct disorders are frequently engaged in bullying, or fighting with others, and are at risk of getting into trouble at school or with the police. Children with ADHD—with hyperactivity exhibit more conduct problems than children with ADHD- without hyperactivity (Barkley et al., 1990; Hynd et al., 1991; Lahey et al., 1984). These problems include aggression (Edelbrock et al., 1984) and generally disruptive behaviours (Stanford & Hynd, 1994). Children with ADHD-inattentiveness, are less aggressive and more compliant home and in school, than children with ADHD-hyperactivity (Barkley et al., 1990). Only in the presence of hyperactive behaviour is inattentive behaviour associated with concurrent conduct problems (Barkley et al., 1990; Goodyear & Hynd, 1992; Warner-Rogers et al., 2000).

Children with ADHD, mostly boys, have oppositional defiant disorder (ODD). These youngsters are often defiant, non-compliant, and have temper outbursts.

The internalizing disorders which co-occur with ADHD are depression, anxiety, and mood disorders (Jensen, Shervette, Xenakis, and Richters, 1993; Tannock, 2000). Females diagnosed with ADHD have more internalizing problems (eg. depression and anxiety) in comparison to males with ADHD (Gaub & Carlson, 1997a; Gershon, 2002). Thus gender differences have been reported in comorbid conditions.

Bipolar disorder also accompanies ADHD in some children. The children exhibit characteristic swing in mood from intense highs to intense lows. There is chronic mood dysregulation with a mixture of elation, depression and irritability (Lowe & Reynolds 2000).

Children with comorbid ADHD and LD manifest more socio-emotional and behavioural difficulties than do their typically developing peers (Al-Yagon, 2009). These children with comorbidity for ADHD and LD reportedly have higher loneliness, lower sense of coherence, lower feelings of hope, and lower effort levels to accomplish tasks, compared with their typically developing peers (Al-Yagon, 2009). The externalizing and internalizing problems of children with comorbid ADHD and LD are rated significantly highly even by their parents in comparison to those of children with typical development (Al-Yagon, 2009).

In addition, children with comorbid ADHD and LD or only with ADHD reportedly have lower attachment security in comparison to their typically developing peers (Al-Yagon, 2009; Clarke et al. 2002 cited in Al-Yagon, 2009). It has been found that children with ADHD are less likely to report secure attachment with mothers as compared with their non-ADHD peers (Clarke et al. 2002, cited in Al-yagon, 2009).

Factors Associated with Socio-emotional and Behavioural Impairment

The increased number of the socio-emotional risk factors experienced by children with comorbid ADHD and LD, alongwith the parents' psychological risk factors contribute and even predict such children's well adjusted functioning (Al-Yagon, 2009).

Parental affect is an important psychological factor which is associated with children's maladjusted behaviours (Goodman & Gotlib, 2002; Zahn-Waxler, Duggal and Gruber, 2002, cited in Al-Yagon, 2009). The parents' affect contributes to the adjustment of children with comorbid ADHD and LD (Al-Yagon, 2009). The inner feelings and overt behaviours of parents which may be positive or negative have the potential to affect adjustment of their children. Thus parents' self-confidence, guilt feeling, worry, depression and anxiety (inner feelings) and overt behaviours such as coping strategies, friendly and energetic behaviour influence their (comorbid ADHD & LD children's) socio-emotional adjustment (Al-Yagon, 2009).

In addition secure attachment of a child with parents is important for well adjusted functioning. Insecure attachment of children plays a role of risk factor for emotional and social maladjustment (Al-Yagon & Mikulincer, 2004). The study of Al-Yagon, 2009 indicates that the socio-emotional problems of children with comorbid ADHD and LD are due to insecure attachment with their parents. The recent growing literature on children with a high incidence of disabilities, show the beneficial effects of secure attachment with mothers in these children's socio-emotional and behavioural attachment (Al-Yagon 2003, 2007, cited in Al-Yagon, 2009; Murray and Pianta, 2007; Al-Yagon, 2009).

The other factor that affects the well adjusted functioning of children with ADHD or comorbid ADHD is the internal neurological factors. Thus neurological problems such as information processing disorders or impulsivity are responsible for these children's social and emotional misperceptions and interpretations, which in turn may impair their social, emotional and behavioural skills (Spafford and Grosser, 1993, cited in Al-Yagon, 2009) thereby affecting their well adjusted functioning.

(3) Social impairments : Children with ADHD also show marked impairment in social functioning. They have low levels of social skills like handling interpersonal conflict or maintaining relationships (Mayes, Calhoun, & Crowell, 2000). They have poor peer relationships and misinterpret social cues (Barkley, 1998b). Studies indicate that children with ADHD have few dyadic friendships, are more often categorized with a rejected social status (Hoza et al., 2005) and are less likely to have secure attachment with significant others (Clarke et al., 2002). Those with ADHD-hyperactivity have been identified as more aggressive towards peers Lahey et al., 1987, and more unpopular (Edelbrock et al., 1984). In comparison, children with ADHD without hyperactivity have been identified to be more socially withdrawn (Edelbrock et al., 1984).They are more likely to be aggressive toward their peers, which in turn leads to peer rejection (Lowe & Reynolds 2000). Impairment in social functioning is also seen when they become adolescents (Greene, Biederman, Faraone, Sienna & Garcia-Jetton, 1997).

Their relationship with adults is also a difficult one. With regard to family relationship, ADHD children show less compliance and more opposition to their parents than non-ADHD children (Kendall, 2000). They do not comply to the requests of parents and teachers. They receive more of commands, reprimands and punishment (Barkley, 1998b).

Prevalence

It is estimated that between 3 per cent to 7 per cent of children have ADHD (American Psychiatric Association, 2000) and the percentage of adults characterized with ADHD is between 2 per cent to 5 per cent (Barkley, 2006). ADHD has been identified in both males and females but is more frequent in males than in females. Among children with ADHD, males manifest more ADHD-related symptoms than do females (Bhatia et al., 1991; Pineda et al., 1999). The male-female ratio of ADHD children ranges from 2:1 to 9:1, depending on the subtype (Gaub & Carlson, 1997b, cited in Lee *et al.*, 2008) and whether the data is from a clinic referred sample (eg. 6:1; Lee *et al.*, 2008) or a random sample (eg., 3.4 : 1; American Psychiatric Association, 2000). Among community-based adults with ADHD symptoms, the men is to women ratio is approximately 2:1 (Murphy & Barkley, 1996). Many researchers have marked that clinic-referred samples are not representative of children with ADHD in general; as the prevalence ratios of boys in clinic-referred samples is much higher than the girls. Girls with ADHD are less likely to be referred to clinic, and are referred, perhaps only when they exhibit most severe problems (Yang et al., 2000).

In addition to difference in gender in prevalence rates, gender differences have been reported in primary ADHD symptoms and comorbid conditions (Gaub & Carlson, 1997a; Gershon, 2002). In comparison to ADHD males, females with ADHD are more likely to display the inattentive subtype of ADHD than the hyperactive-inpulsive and the combined subtype, as per DSM-IV criteria. They (females) are likely to manifest fewer symptoms of hyperactivity, impulsivity and conduct problems (eg. less aggression), and have more internalizing problems (eg., depression, and anxiety) (Lee, Oakland, Jackson & Glutting, 2008, Lahe *et al*, 1998; Wolraich *et al.*, 1996). However no significant gender difference has been reported for self reported ADHD symptoms in college and university students from U.S., Italy and New Zeeland (Du Paul et al., 2001; Heiligenstein et al., 1998). The possible reasons for lack of gender difference in the sample of university students are (DuPaul *et al.*, 2001) :

- Absence of gender differences among higher achieving students who are able to attend post secondary institutions;
- Use of self-report data in contrast to the parent and teacher ratings of symptoms typically obtained with children and adolescents;
- More likelihood for women in general to self-report ADHD symptoms (Compas, 1997).

ADHD is prevalent across nations and cultures, with some cross-national and cross-cultural differences emerging (DuPaul et al., 2001; Kendall, 2000). For example, in U.K. prevalence of ADHD is low (Taylor, 1994), whereas in China there is a high rate of hyperactivity (Luk & Leung, 1989). In U.S., the prevalence rate of all ADHD subtypes is approximately 4 per cent to 5 per cent in adults and university students (Murphy & Barkley, 1996; DuPaul et al., 2001; Heiligenstein, et al., 1998). The prevalence rates in university students of Italy and NewZealand are higher than the expected 3 per cent to 5 per cent as reported by the DSM IV (DuPaul et al., 2001). High percentages of ADHD are also found in India, where 29.2 per cent of children aged 11 to 12 met criteria for ADHD (Bhatia, Nigam, Bohr, & Malik, 1991), and in Germany, where the percentage of ADHD children varied from 9.6 per cent (age 5) to 17.8 per cent (age 17) (Baumgaertel, Wolraich, & Dierrich, 1995; cited in DuPaul et al., 2001). However, interpretations of these rates must be made with caution due to inconsistent diagnostic methods (Mann et al., 1992).

Race differences in ADHD have also been found. There is a higher prevalence of ADHD symptoms in African American children than in Caucasian children (Jarvinen & Sprague, 1995, Reid *et al.*,1998, cited in Lee *et al.*, 2008). Among college students also more African American students (0.9%) have been identified with ADHD than Caucasian students (0.1%) (Lee, Oakland, Jackson & Glutting, 2008). Possible reasons suggested for the racial and cultural differences are :

- African American children are more likely to be exposed to prenatal risk factors, psycho-social stressors and economic disadvantage which in turn adversely affect ADHD behaviours (Reid *et al.*, 1998).
- Parents' expectations of their children's behaviour differ from culture to culture leading to difference in their awareness of ADHD related behaviours, standards for judging its appropriateness and tolerance rates of deviant behaviours. The cultural

variations in the parents' understanding of ADHD related behaviours affect their report of such behaviours (Lee et al., 2008) and availing of health services and interventions for ADHD (Angold et al., 2000; Bussing, Schoenberg, Roger et al., 1998 cited in Lee et al., 2008). African-American parents are less likely to report and show concern for their children's ADHD related emotiona or beahvioural distrubances and school problems (Bussing, Schoenberg, Rogers et al., 1998; Bussing, Schoenberg & Perwien, 1998). On the other hand Chinese parents seem to have low tolerance rates for hyperactive behaviours and so are more likely to report them (Ho et al., 1996, cited in Lee et al., 2008).

- The concept of ADHD and instruments designed to assess it reflect a western perspective, and that neither the concept nor the instruments consider cultural difference (Bird, 2002; Anderson, 1996).

Children with ADHD have been identified from both urban and rural areas and also from high and low socio-economic strata. But there is a somewhat greater frequency of ADHD children from lower socio-economic classes. Possible explanations for this have been suggested which are :

- Pregnant mothers from lower socio-economic status are likely to have poor nutrition and care, and also high incidence of complications, perhaps affecting the brain development of the unborn child. (Biederman *et al.* 1995).
- The troubled environment of low socio-economic status families might account for higher rates of family instability, divorce, and parental psychological disorders (Biederman *et al.* 1995).
- The high incidence of ADHD among low socio-economic class children may be due to biasedness of

teachers and others to expect ADHD behaviour among them (Kendall, 2000).

Prevalence rates for ADHD vary depending on whether they are obtained from self-report, parent report or teacher report. About 7 per cent to 11 per cent difference in prevalence rates has been found with higher rates of ADHD symptoms identified in parent reports than in self-reports (Fischer, 1997, cited in Lee et.al., 2008). Method of assessment leads to variance between parent and teacher ratings of ADHD. Upto 59 per cent of the common variance between parent and teacher ratings of ADHD was found to be due to method of assessment rather than due to trait variance (inattention and hyperactivity-impulsivity traits) (Burns, Walsh & Gomege, 2003).

ADHD Children in Advanced Age

Many professionals prior to the 1970s believed that ADHD symptoms diminished during adolescence and abated by adulthood (Barkley, 2006). There was a belief in people that these children would outgrow their problems without any treatment, but this is not fully true (Kendall, 2000). It has been observed, with regard to prognosis and long-term outcome, that there are some children diagnosed with ADHD who cease to manifest ADHD like symptoms in adult life, or in other words 'outgrow' their deficits (Fischer et al., 1993; Klein & Mannuzza, 1991; Weiss et al., 1985). But, for many, the ADHD symptoms persist and it can be a disorder for life; such children with ADHD continue to exhibit symptoms significantly throughout adolescence and also in early adulthood (Barkley, Fischer, Smallish & Fletcher, 2002; Mannuzza & Klein, 2000). Estimates suggest that upto two-thirds of children diagnosed with ADHD will continue to exhibit symptoms into adulthood (Resnick, 2005), this is confirmed in longitudinal researches. Six to twelve year-old children with ADHD, who were followed for 10 to 25 years in various studies, nearly two-thirds continued to manifest at least one of the disabling symptoms of ADHD (i.e., inattention, hyperactivity, impulsivity) as adolescents and adults (Gittleman, Mannuzza, Shenker & Bonagura, 1985; Weiss & Hechtman, 1993, cited in Frazier et al., 2007). It is suggested that those individuals who outgrow their ADHD do so because they are able to 'seek out' and create environments correlated with their genetic propensities (Plomin, 1999). There is a likelihood that they seek out environments that do not expose their executive function weaknesses required in the adaptations to the environment and elementary problem solving components (Schuck & Crinella, 2005).

Symptoms of ADHD change somewhat from childhood to adolescence. There is a decline in excessive motor activity and impulsive symptoms in adolescence but the other problems of ADHD seem to persist (Cantwell, 1987; Weiss & Hechtman, 1986, cited in Kendall, 2000; Hart et al., 1995). Symptoms of inattention seem to remain relatively stable. Literature suggests that with age hyperactive impulsive symptoms subside more than the inattentive symptoms within individuals with ADHD, (Biederman, Mick & Faraone, 2000).

As said, overt hyperactivity diminishes but internal or mental restlessness seems to remain within the individuals with ADHD. Symptoms of internal restlessness rather than overt hyperactivity are likely to be reported by adolescents and adults (Weyandt et al., 2003). They are more likely to display difficulties with internal distractions, for example, day-dreaming, or a constant flow of task relevant and irrelevant ideas (Conners et al., 1999; Downey, Stelson, Pomerleau, & Giordani, 1997; Weyandt et al., 2003).

Academic problems, with regard to age, appear to extend beyond childhood, being also of consequence for adolescents, college students, and adults who either were first diagnosed with ADHD during childhood or for whom symptoms were recognized later (Frazier et al., 2004). Similarly social problems also extend beyond childhood. The problems of attentional focus and related academic difficulties and social difficulties continue into adolescence in approximately 50 to 75 per cent of individuals with ADHD (Fischer, Barkley, Edelbrock, & Smallish, 1990; Gittleman, Mannuzza, Shenker & Bonagura, 1985, cited in Kendall, 2000) and potentially into adulthood (Kendall, 2000).

In a retrospective study adults with ADHD were found to have obtained less formal education or lower grades while in high school (Barkley, Fischer, Smallish & Fletcher, 2002). Even though the academic difficulties continue to persist in adulthood, there is a trend toward decreasing academic impairment with age (Frazier et al., 2007). This is probably because children with high ADHD impairments do not pursue education till school or beyond it. It may also be due to the reason that individuals with ADHD learn more about their problems and compensate by checking their work, re-reading their passages or seeking additional instruction. Or else, a decline in ADHD symptoms (hyperactive impulsive symptoms) with age may result in fewer achievement problems among adolescents and adults (Frazier et al., 2007). In few studies done exclusively on college students (e.g. Konold & Glutting, 2008; Glutting, Monaghan et al., 2002), they were found to have higher ability levels, greater academic success during primary and secondary school, and better compensatory skills than individuals with ADHD from the general population.

The persisting ADHD problems into adolescence and adulthood are sometimes also associated with other comorbid diagnoses suggesting that the decline in symptoms does not indicate a decline in risk. These diagnoses include conduct disorder, mood disorders, disruptive behaviours, oppositional behaviour, learning disabilities, substance abuse, severe antisocial personality disorder, and poor family relations (Farrington, 1991; Kandel et al., 1988, Seguin, Pihl, Harden, Tremblay, & Boulerice, 1995). College students with ADHD are more likely to experience difficulties in anger control and anger expression when faced with psychological distress (Ramirez et al., 1997; Richards, Deffenbacher, Rose'n, 2002).

It is suggested from existing prevalence data that 2 per cent to 5 per cent of the general population continue to display appreciable ADHD symptoms into adult life (Barkley, 2006). To know the exact adult prevalence further research is required. On college campuses, ADHD tends to be under diagnosed and misdiagnosed (Reilley, 2005). Less is known about ADHD at the college level than children, adolescent or adults (Du Paul et al., 2001; Heiligenstein, Guenther, Levy, Savino & Fulwiler, 1999).

Surely, the distractibility, inattentiveness, and difficulties with goal directed persistence remain a serious problem with many of the adults with past record of ADHD (Biederman et al., 1993; Spencer et al., 1994, cited in Kendall, 2000).

SUMMARY

Attention deficit hyperactivity disorder (ADHD) is a disorder with characteristic behaviour pattern of hyperactivity, impulsivity, and/or inattention. These behaviours are displayed at developmentally inappropriate levels, and appear early in life in the preschool and early school years. ADHD was first described by Dr. Heinrich Hoffman in 1845. Later in 1902 Sir George F. Still made recognition of ADHD easier. The conceptualization of attention deficit hyperactivity disorder and its terminology have undergone several revisions during three decades from 1960s to 1990s in DSM and ICD. The DSM-IV-TR requires at least six symptoms each of inattention and hyperactivity/impulsivity for diagnosis of ADHD. Three subtypes of ADHD are recognized: (1) predominantly inattentive type; (2) predominantly hyperactive impulsive type; and (3) combined type. Children with predominantly inattentive type of ADHD are rarely impulsive or hyperactive, but they have significant problems paying attention. Children with predominantly hyperactive and impulsive type of ADHD do not show significant inattention, but have impaired performance on tasks requiring behavioural inhibition. Children with combined type of ADHD exhibit both inattentiveness and impulsive hyperactive behaviour in significant manner. ADHD, quite commonly, exists with other difficulties and disorders such as learning disability, socio-emotional and behavioural impairement and social impairements. It is estimated that 3 to 7 per cent of children and 2 to 5 per cent of adults have ADHD. It is more frequent in males than in females, the ratio ranging from 2:1 to 9:1 depending on the subtype and sample (clinic or community based). ADHD is prevalent across nations and cultures with some cross-national and cross-cultural differences emerging. Prevalence rates vary depending upon use of self-report, parent report or teacher report. The problems associated with this disorder often continue into adolescence and adulthood.

Chapter 2

Characteristics

Cognitive Functioning

Individuals with ADHD have difficulties in cognitive processes. They are more likely to be behind in aspects of cognitive functioning in comparison to their peer groups. The cognitive processes include executive function, attention, and memory. The cognitive processes controlled by central executive system or executive functions are likely to be dysfunctional. Intelligence in ADHD population is more or less similar to the general population barring very high intelligence which is not a typical feature of ADHD.

Executive Function

The major cognitive deficit of children with ADHD is impaired executive system. Rather, executive function deficit is considered to be the core feature of ADHD (e.g., Barkley, 1997b; Denckla, 1995; Douglas, 1988; Seidman et al., 1997). However, it is not the sole feature representing ADHD, other deficits in cognitive processes may also underlie the disorder (Tsal, Shalev & Mevorach, 2005).

A particular set of components or computational subroutines operate during mental activity, such as problem solving, and exert superordinate control over the brain's computational programmes (Sternberg, 1985). These set of components or computational subroutines are known as executive functions. The other various terms for executive functions are 'executive processes', 'executive routines', 'control processes', or 'meta components' (Schuck & Crinella, 2005).

The executive system (also referred to as central executive) is considered to be primarily responsible for co-ordinating activity within the cognitive system. Besides this, it also devotes some of its resources to increasing the amount of information that can be held in the memory storage systems (Baddeley & Logie, 1999).

Executive function (EF) processes, according to Sternberg (1984), include: (*i*) decision as to just what the problem is that needs to be solved; (*ii*) selection of lower order components; (*iii*) selection of one or more representations or organizations of information; (*iv*) selection of a strategy for combining lower order components; (*v*) decision regarding trade-offs in the speed and accuracies with which various components are executed; and (*vi*) solution monitoring. Other lists of EF components abound (e.g., Schuck & Crinella, 2005; Barkley, 1997b; Fletcher, 1996; Welsh & Pennington, 1988) which include: (*vii*) planning; (*viii*) simultaneous and sequential processing; (*ix*) working memory; (*x*) self-regulation of affect, motivation and arousal; (*xi*) internalization of speech; (*xii*) analysis and synthesis of behaviour; (*xiii*) set shifting; (*xiv*) set maintenance; and (*xv*) impulse control. EF has also a role in some attentional processes (Posner & Raichle, 1994, cited in Schuck & Crinella, 2005). Executive function (EF) involves "the 'where' or 'whether' aspects of behaviour, while non-executive functions involve the 'what' and 'how' " (Barkley, 2000a, p. 1065).

Any act of problem solving requires EF, irrespective of the number, type, or computational power of the discrete subroutines executed within the brain's neural networks (Schuck & Crinella, 2005).

Problems with executive functions are common in ADHD. Examples of executive function deficits are : children with ADHD display difficulties with planning, organizing tasks and activities, monitoring and checking task performance (Barkley, 1995; Seidman et al., 2001, cited in Re, Pedron & Cornoldi, 2007), difficulties with attentional switching/control (Preston et al., 2009), difficulties with non-verbal and verbal working memory tasks (Barkley, 1998b).

Other cognitive deficits in ADHD are concerned with goal-related behaviours. Children with ADHD have problems in establishing goals, holding goals in memory, making persistent efforts towards goals, and shaping and redirecting behaviours in order to achieve goals (Barkley, 1997, cited in Lienemann & Reid, 2008).

According to Barkley (1997b), executive function (EF) is absolutely necessary for goal attainment, because it is composed of cognitive subcomponents such as prolongation of action, separation of affect, guidance by inner language, and analysis/synthesis of action. Barkley, (1997b) conceptualized that inhibition—the ability to stop or delay responding for periods of time—accounts for virtually all of the classical ADHD symptoms (e.g., impulsivity, distractibility, diminished persistence, diminished sensitivity to feedback, lack of planning and judgement, and poor modulation of affect). Thus, ADHD involves problems with behavioural inhibition and self-control, which is associated with poor executive function (EF) control (Barkley, 1997b). Sandberg, Day, and Trott (1996), pointed out that ADHD is mainly caused by cognitive deficits in controlling the processes of self-regulation and inhibition. Stressing on gravity of executive function deficits, Schuck & Crinella (2005), state that, "In truth, the most worrisome deficits of children with ADHD are not the product of low IQ, but rather of the instability of control processes that govern everyday adaptations to the environment" (p. 275).

Children with ADHD may also have a poor sense of time, reduced sensitivity to error, difficulty with simultaneous and sequential tasks (Barkley, 1998b) which again indicates deficits in executive cognitive functioning. Deficits in executive function in these children negatively affect their academic performance (Clark, Prior & Kinsella, 2002).

Studies show that in comparison to typical children, children with ADHD lag behind in executive function processes. Children with ADHD differ from typically developing children in their selection of responses and their ability to suppress or postpone a response (Van der Meere, 1996), as well as in other executive functions such as planning. Van Luit, Kroesbergen & Naglieri (2005) found that children with ADHD had low scores on planning and attention than typical children.

Measures of Executive Function

The two measures of executive functions are *Continuous Performance Test* (CPT; Conners, 1992) and *Wisconsin Card Sorting Test* (WCST; Heaton, 1981). These are commonly in use for investigating executive functions components (e.g., Schuck & Crinella, 2005; Pennington et al., 1993; Reader et al., 1994). Both the CPT and the WCST are administered on computer. Schuck & Crinella (2005) used CPT in their study specifically to probe the capacity to control impulsive errors (IMPULS). They used WCST specifically to assess two other aspects of executive functions, the ability to shift cognitive sets (via inhibition of perseverative tendencies; PERSEV) and the ability to maintain set (FAIL-SET). The version of CPT and WCST used in laboratory by Schuck & Crinella is presented hereafter.

CPT

The child is seated before the computer display screen and instructed to press the space bar as quickly as possible when any letter, except X, flashes on the screen. When the letter X appears, the response (pressing the space bar) is to be withheld. The letter X is presented randomly on the computer screen, for example, two times in a trial. For all letters, the display time is 250 ms. The time intervals between two letters presented on the screen, i.e., inter stimulus intervals (ISIs) are either 1, 2 or 4 seconds. A total of 360 letter presentations occur, divided into six blocks of 60; within each block 20 consecutive trials are given for each of the three ISIs (Schuck & Crinella, 2005). The task requires a total of 15 minutes. The dependent variable which is of interest is impulsive errors (IMPULS; i.e., key presses when the non-target X appears on the computer screen).

The CPT version used by Schuck & Crinella (2005) is more or less 'pure' test of impulse control, having very little to do with understanding complex rules or retaining significant amounts of information in working memory.

WCST

The participant child is seated before the computer display screen and instructed to match cards that appear on the screen with stationery cards that remain on the screen. Four sample cards remain stationery on the screen. The sample cards can be categorized by colour (red, green, blue or yellow), form (crosses, circles, squares, or triangles) and numbers (one, two, three or four). There are a series of 128 single stimulus cards to be matched with one of the four sample cards. The stimulus cards appear one at a time on the screen and the participant has to match each stimulus card with one of the four sample cards on the screen. The participant is not informed of the relevant category, only the computer gives signals of 'right' by the sound of bell or 'wrong' by the sound of buzzer after each response.

The test proceeds through unannounced shifts among three possible sorting categories (colour, form, and number), with each shift occurring only after 10 of 10 consecutive correct matching responses. In this test two variables are measured. First, the perseverative errors (PERSEV), i.e., matching a card using the previously correct but now incorrect category, are measured. Second, failure to *maintain set* (FAILSET) is taken into account i.e., failure to persist with the criterion of 10 of 10 consecutive correct responses after 4 consecutive correct responses have been achieved.

Attention

Attention is an important cognitive function, and more so, for understanding of ADHD. Cognitive deficits in attentional function are important feature of ADHD. It is conceptualized to be a complex, multidimensional concept with each domain having different function. The number of domains within attentional system differs according to its conceptualization by the researchers. Three separate domains of attention have been most commonly described (e.g. Parasuraman, 2000) : (1) sustained attention; (2) selective attention; and (3) executive attention. Attention system comprising of four domains, each with distinct function have also been suggested (Tsal, Shalev, & Mevorach, 2005) : (1) sustained attention; (2) selective attention; (3) orienting attention; and (4) executive attention. Very recently Preston et al. (2009) conceptualized of three domains of attention: (1) sustained attention; (2) selective attention; and (3) attentional switching/control. The functions of these attention domains are :

(1) ***Sustained attention :*** It involves maintaining attention over an extended period of time;

(2) ***Selective attention :*** It involves attending to relevant stimuli/information while effectively ignoring irrelevant stimuli/information;

(3) ***Attentional switching/control :*** It involves executive functioning skills. Attentional switching is concerned

with the skill or ability to change focus flexibly and adaptively (Cooley & Morris, 1990; Mirsky, Anthony, Duncan, Dhearn, & Kellam, 1991; Sergeant & van der Meere, 1990; cited in Preston et al., 2009), ie. redirecting momentarily focussed attention to a different location in space (Posner Inhoff, Friedrich & Cohen, 1987). This attentional switching is also referred as orienting attention by Tsal, Shalev & Mevorach (2005), or attentional disengagement by Posner et al. (1987). Attentional control involves the skill or ability to inhibit responses to irrelevant stimuli or automatic responses and initiate more relevant alternative responses (Anderson, 2002; Baddeley 1986). This dimension/domain of attentional switching/control requires more executive control than the other dimensions/domains. It represents the domain that orchestrates and directs other higher order cognitive processes.

The distinct functions of sustaining attention and selective attention have been described in almost similar way in various conceptualizations. Selective attention and orienting of attention have sometimes been used interchangeably in the literature. But recently, either the two have been included as separate dimensions due to distinct different functions (e.g Tsal, Shalev & Mevorach, 2005) or orienting of attention is included in executive attentional dimension (e.g. Preston et al., 2009).

The function of executive attention described by Tsal, Shalev and Mevorach (2005), as 'inhibiting responses to irrelevant stimuli', is similar to that of Preston et al's attentional control. Similarly the function of orienting attention described by Tsal et al. as 'directing attention to a designated location and reorienting to a new location', is more are less similar to that of attentional switching of Preston et al. In children with ADHD, attentional switching/control is an integral component to reading, math and spelling success (Preston et al., 2009).

Children with ADHD exhibit a variety of attention problems reflecting deficits in various domains of attentional functions. ADHD children with inattentive and combined subtypes have been found to exhibit various deficits in sustained attention, selective attention, orienting of attention and executive attention (Tsal, Shalev & Mevorach, 2005). These children experience much deficits in sustained attention (Aylward, Gordon & Verhulst, 1997; Preston et al. 2009) and attentional switching/control (Preston et al., 2009) and less deficit in selective attention (Preston et al., 2009)

The most prevalent attention deficits (of children with ADHD) is in the domain of sustained attention (Tsal, Shalev & Mevorach, 2005). Considering the two subtypes of ADHD, it has been found that children with ADHD combined subtype and children with inattentive subtype, do not differ in the overall construct of attention (Preston et al., 2009), or in any of the domains of attention (Tsal, Shalev & Mevorach, 2005). The inattentive and combined subtypes although markedly differing in symptoms of hyperactivity and impulsivity, still possess similar deficits in attentional functions (Tsal, Shalev & Mevorach, 2005).

But children with ADHD do differ among themselves with respect to deficits in the different attentional functions. Different children with ADHD manifest divergent combinations of attention deficits. They may have deficit in any one or in any combination of the various attentional functions. For example, it has been found in the study of Tsal, shalev and Mevorach (2005) that some children with ADHD manifest attentional deficit in only one function or domain and most have deficits in two or three domains. Thus, not all children clinically diagnosed with ADHD are alike in their attention, and are likely to show different deficits in the various attentional functions of sustained, selective and executive attention.

There is behavioural evidence (from attentional tasks) as well as neuro-physiological evidence (from brain abnormalities) which suggest that the performance of children with ADHD is inferior to that of control children in sustained attention (Richards et al., 1990; Scahill & Schwab-Stone, 2000; Taranowski et al., 1986), selective attention (Richards et al., 1990; Shalev & Tsal, 2003; Taranowski et al., 1986), orienting of attention (Filipek et al., 1997, Hynd et al., 1991; Nigg et al., 1997) and executive attention (Barkley et al., 1992; Schachar & Logan, 1990). Richards et al. (1990) showed that the children with ADHD performed in less efficient manner than the control group in sustained attention using the Continuous Performance Test (CPT). There was no evidence for the deterioration of performance over time. The difficulty in selective attention task was most prominent when the distance between the target and the distractors was small. This is an indication that children with ADHD have impairment in their ability to focus attention on a relatively small area in the visual field, which is the characteristic of an earlier developmental stage in typical children (Pasto & Burack, 1997). Jonkman et al. (1999) compared children with ADHD and typical control children with respect to their ability to focus on a target stimulus and ignore two distractors that flanked the target (i.e., selective attention). They found that children with ADHD made more errors to incongruent stimuli than control children. However no differences in reaction time were found for correct responses between children with ADHD and control children. Another study suggested that one of the deficits of children with ADHD is the inability to restrict visual attention to a limited spatial area (i.e., sustained attention) so as to selectively process relevant information while effectively ignoring distracting information (Shalev & Tsal, 2003) .

The DSM-IV diagnosis of ADHD treats attention as a single, undifferentiated entity, though neuro-psychological and behavioural research point to the existence of several separate attention systems (Tsal, Shalev & Mevorach, 2005). Various children with ADHD can have different deficits in the various attentional functions. Since, they are diagnosed with ADHD when scoring high on any six of the nine symptoms of inattention on the list of inattention scale of DSM-IV, they cannot be grouped into homogenous clusters with same domain of attention. Different tests of attention for different domains could delineate the unique attentional profile of each child with ADHD. Thereafter, children with relatively homogenous clusters of symptoms in a given domain of attention could be evolved for providing intervention appropriate for them. It has been proposed by Swanson et al. (2000) that the various DSM-IV symptoms used to diagnose ADHD could be divided into subgroups uniquely characterizing sustained attention, orienting of attention, and executive attention. However, future research is needed to correlate various symptoms of ADHD with these unique deficits in different attention functions, which is also suggested by some researchers (eg. Tsal et al., 2005).

Measures of Attention

There are various tests for measuring different dimensions of attention. Some of these are described here in brief for clarity:

Sustained Attention

Vigilance task (Tsal, Shalev & Mevorach, 2005) is in use for measuring sustained attention. In this task participants are presented with a long series of stimuli and they respond to a prespecified target while withholding responses to all other, non-target stimuli. Variance in response times to the target as well as errors of omission and commission serve as measures of lapses in sustained attention. The vigilance task is similar to *Continuous Performance Test* (CPT, e.g. Rosvold, Mirsky, Sarason, Bransome, & Beck, 1956).

Selective Attention

It is measured using conjunctive search task (Treisman & Gelade, 1980; Tsal, Shalev & Mevorach, 2005). Participants search for a blue square appearing on the background of a variable number of red squares and blue circles. Reduction in performance as a function of increased display size serves as a measure of selective attention deficits.

Executive Attention

Stroop-like task (Stroop, 1935) is used for measuring executive attention (Tsal, Shalev & Mevorach, 2005). Participants respond 'up' or 'down' to an arrow located either above or below fixation and pointing either upward or downward. In one condition they respond to the location of the arrow and in the other condition, they respond to its direction. The interference produced by the dimension to be ignored is measured by comparing respond for congruent and incongruent displays.

Apart from these measures, there is a single measure or test that assesses multiple domains of attention. This is *Test of Everyday Attention for children* (TEA-Ch; Manly, Robertson, Anderson & Nimmo-Smith, 1999). It consists of nine subtests which involve game-like tasks for sustained attention, selective attention, and attentional switching/control. These subtests are mentioned hereafter :

Sustained attention is assessed by five subtests of TEA-Ch. These are :

1. *Score !* : It involves a task of auditory attention to tones.
2. *Score ! DT* : It is a dual auditory task requiring the participant to count tones while listening for an animal name in a 'news report'.
3. *Sky Search DT* : It is multimodal dual task requiring the participant to identify visual target while counting tones.
4. *Walk, Don't Walk* : It is a test of auditory attention requiring the participant to mark steps that correspond to a target sound while inhibiting response to a non-target sound.

5. *Code Transmission* : It is also a auditory attention test that requires the participant to identify the number that follows a specific sequence, such as the number following two consecutive '3s'.

Selective Attention is assessed by two subtests of TEA-Ch:

1. *Sky Search* (Attention score); and
2. *Map Mission*

Both of these tests involve rapidly identifying visual targets among distractors.

Attentional Switching/control is measured by two subtests of TEA-Ch :

1. *Creature Counting* : It involves rapid switching between counting forward and backward in response to visual stimuli. In this subtest timing is scored. It is similar to stroop tasks (Stroop, 1935) used for measuring executive attention;
2. *Opposite Worlds* : It involves rapid cognitive reversal of an overlearned response; eg. saying 1 while seeing 2. In this, opposit world is scored.

It has been suggested by Preston et al., 2009 that tests of attention, specifically those that utilize attentional switching/control, may be useful tools in predicting difficulties in academic performance.

MEMORY

Working Memory

ADHD is characterized by difficulties with inhibiting behaviour (Barkley, 1997b) that trigger secondary effects in executive functions like working memory (Van Mourick, Oosterlaan, & Sergeant, 2005; Willcutt, Pennington, Olson, Chhabildas, & Hulslander, 2005). Working memory is the ability to store and manipulate information for brief periods (Alloway, Rajendran & Archibald, 2009). Working memory is defined as a processing resource of limited capacity, which is involved in the preservation of information while processing the same or other information (Baddeley & Logie, 1999; Unsworth & Engle, 2007 cited in Swanson, Zheng & Jerman, 2009). Working memory is not a single store but a memory system consisting of separable interacting components. These components function in concert and provide a kind of flexible mental workspace which can be used to maintain and transform information in the course of demanding cognitive activities (Alloway & Archibald, 2008).

Several theories about working memory exist. One of the theoretical models, which is widely used, is that of Baddeley & Hitch (1974). This model suggests that there are separable components for the temporal storage of verbal and visuospatial information—the phonological loop and the visuospatial sketchpad respectively. A centralized component (executive system) co-ordinates the flow of information between these storage systems, and temporarily activates long-term memory. The central executive system also functions as a mental workspace involved in the temporary storage and manipulation of information needed in the execution of complex cognitive tasks, like, learning, reasoning, and comprehension (Alloway & Archibald, 2008).

Tasks that measure working memory assess an individual's ability to maintain task-relevant information and ignore or inhibit other information as they complete task-relevant operations. Examples of everyday working memory tasks are: (*i*) holding a person's address in mind while listening to instructions about how to get there; (*ii*) listening to a sequence of events in a story while trying to understand what the story means (Swanson, Zheng & Jerman 2009). The working memory tasks place heavy demands on an executive system and tap mental resources (Cowan, 1995, cited in Swanson, Zheng and Jerman, 2009). Controlled processing on working memory emerges when resources have to be drawn directly from the central executive system. Also, when demands are high on attention for example, when a memory trace has to be maintained in the face of interference, controlled processing on working memory is invoked. A child with working memory deficits has to struggle to hold in mind and manipulate relevant information in the course of ongoing mental activities.

Working memory ability is a key component in learning during development (Gathercole et al., 2006; Swanson & Sachse-Lee, 2001).

It has been demonstrated that children with ADHD have poorer working memory than those in control groups (Barkley 1997b; McInnes *et al.* 2003). Children with the combined subtype of ADHD have been specifically studied and found to have poorer working memory than the control group (Jacobson and Kikas, 2007). Furthermore, children having both ADHD and learning disability, show considerably poorer performance in memory tasks than those with 'pure' ADHD (Johnson, Altmaier, & Richman, 1999, Shin *et al.* 2003). Working memory deficits are found in ADHD children across both verbal and visuospatial domains (Alloway, Rajendran, & Archibald, 2009) with a tendency for more deficits in visuospatial memory than verbal ones (Martinussen, Hayden, Hogg, Johnson & Tannock, 2005). Children with ADHD perform poorly in the visuo-spatial tasks such as copying figures. The figures copied by them were found to be significantly less organized than those of control group children on the Ray-Osterrieth Complex Figure test (Grodzinsky & Diamond, 1992; Shin, Kim, Cho & Kim, 2003).

Short-term Memory

Short-term memory is the ability to hold small amounts of information passively and then producing it in an untransformed fashion (Swanson, Zheng & Jerman, 2009). Tasks that measure short-term memory, do not require the individuals to infer, transform or vary processing requirements. They are simply asked to recall a sequence of items in the order in which they were presented in front of them. Examples of short-term memory tasks are forward recall of letters, digits, words and spatial locations. The short term memory tasks do not rely on the central executive system as working memory tasks (e.g. Cowan, 1995, cited in Swanson, Zheng & Jerman, 2009). In contrast to working memory, controlled processing on short-term memory tasks emerges when memory traces have to be maintained above some critical threshold (Cowan, 1995). Unlike working memory, resources are not drawn directly from the central executive system in this maintenance (Swanson, Zheng & Jerman, 2009).

Short-term memory of children with ADHD is at par with age-expected levels (Roodenrys, 2006). But Jacobson and Kikas, 2007 have found that word memory and memory for objects is poorer in children with ADHD-combind subtype, than the control group.

Causes of Poor Memory

Poor working memory, according to one theory is not because of working memory deficit per se, but possibly due to these children's difficulty in regulating their own behaviour which interferes with attending to the information presented to them (Alloway, Rajendran & Archibald, 2009). This notion gets support from research where scores on working memory improved as a result of medication to regulate behaviour and maintain focus (Mehta *et al.*, 2004).

Working memory performance is also influenced by the meaningfulness of the task. When memory tasks are semantically and spatially meaningful, the performance of children with ADHD may be similar to that of children without disabilities (Adams *et al.*, 1991). The concreteness and meanigfulness of the task seemed to help children with ADHD combind subtype but it did not always help children with ADHD-combined subtype with comorbid learning disability (Jacobson & Kikas, 2007).

Children with ADHD get easily distracted by irrelevant stimuli. Distraction of stimuli and poor ability to relate objects to each other hampers their concurrent visual processing ability (Jacobson & Kikas, 2007). This results in poorer performance in the non-verbal memory tasks in children with ADHD-combined subtype, than the control group (Jacobson & Kikas, 2007). Weaker performance in the memory for objects task show that these children are not able to distinguish preselected objects among a number of distracting objects (Jacobson & Kikas, 2007). The poorer performance on both these tasks could be due to weaker problem solving skills, such as the inability to use landmarks to memorize the position (Jacobson & Kikas, 2007).

Measures of Memory Assessment

A test battery which has been used for assessing memory of children with ADHD is *Automated Working Memory Assessment* (AWMA, Alloway, 2007) (Alloway & Archibald, 2008). It consists of following tests :

1. ***Verbal short-term memory measures :*** There are three verbal short-term memory measures which are: (*i*) digit recall; (*ii*) word recall; and (*iii*) non-word recall. In each test, a sequence of verbal items (digits, one-syllable words, and one-syllable nonwords, respectively) are presented and the individual is required to recall each sequence in the correct order. Digit lists are random constructions without replacement from the digits ranging from 1 to 9, spoken at a rate of one digit per second. The word lists are monosyllabic words with a consonant-vowel-consonant structure, and no stimuli are repeated. The non-words have the same structure and are created using the same pool of phonemes as the words used in the word recall subtests. The words and non-words, which are spoken at a rate of one syllable per second, must be recalled with full accuracy (i.e., with all three phonemes correct) and in the correct serial position. Credit is given for phoneme substitutions when the

substitution constituted the child's habitual articulation pattern for that phoneme.

2. ***Verbal working memory measures*** : There are three verbal working memory measures, which are: (*i*) listening recall; (*ii*) backward digit recall; and (*iii*) counting recall. In the listening recall test, a child is presented with a series of spoken sentences (e.g., 'Lions have four legs', 'Pineapples play football') and has to verify the sentence by stating 'true' or 'false' and recall the final word for each sentence in sequence. Test trials begin with one sentence and continue with additional sentences in each block until the child is unable to recall three correct trials at a block. In the backward digit recall test, a child is required to recall a sequence of spoken digits in the reverse order. Test trials begin with two numbers and increase by one number in each block until the child is unable to recall four correct trails at a particular block. In the counting recall test, the child is presented with a visual array of red circles and blue triangles. He or she is required to count the number of circles in an array and then recall the tallies of circles in the arrays that were presented. The test trial begins with one visual array and increases by an additional visual array in each block until the child is unable to correctly recall four trials. Each visual array stays on the screen until the child indicates that he or she has completed counting all the circles. The number of correct trials are scored for each child.

3. ***Visuospatial short-term memory*** : There are three measures of visuospatial short-term memory. These are: (*i*) block recall test; (*ii*) mazes memory test; and (*iii*) dot matrix task. In the block recall test, the child views a video of a series of blocks being tapped. In fact, the presenter taps a sequence of cubes with a finger on a specifically designed board that has nine

randomly located cubes. The child's task is to repeat the sequence in the same order. Testing begins with a single block tap and increases by one additional block. In the mazes memory test, the child is shown for 3 seconds a two dimensional line maze with a red path drawn through maze. The same maze is then shown to the child without the path, and the child is asked to recall the path by drawing it on the maze. In the dot matrix task, a sequence of red dots is presented on a 4×4 grid, and the child is required to point to the positions of each dot that had appeared in the sequence in the same order. Each dot appears for 2 seconds. The sequences are random, with no location being highlighted more than once within a trial.

4. ***Visuospatial working memory test :*** There are three measures of visuospatial working memory. These are: (*i*) odd-one-out task; (*ii*) Mr. X task; and (*iii*) spatial span task. In the odd one out task, a child views a horizontal row of three boxes in which three complex shapes are presented. The child has to point to the shape that does not match the others and remembers its location. At the end of the trial, a blank set of three boxes appears on the screen. The child points to the boxes in which the odd shapes had appeared in the correct order. The boxes always appear horizontally on the screen, but at different positions along the vertical axis to eliminate visual traces.

In the Mr. X task, a child is presented with a picture of two Mr. X figures. The child identifies whether the Mr. X with the blue hat is holding the ball in the same hand as the Mr. X with the yellow hat. The Mr. X with blue hat may also be rotated. At the end of each trial, the child has to recall the location of each ball in the blue Mr. X's hand in sequence, by pointing to a picture with eight compass points. Both the Mr. X figures and the compass point stay on the computer screen until the child provides a response.

In the spatial span task, a child views a picture of two identical shapes in which the shape on the right has a red dot on it. The child identifies whether the shape on the right is the same or opposite of the shape on the left. The shape with the red dot may also be rotated. At the end of each trial, the child has to recall the location of each red dot on the shape in sequence, by pointing to a picture with three compass points. Both the shapes and compass points stay on the computer screen until the child provides a response.

Another test battery for assessing memory is working memory test battery for children (WMTB-C, Pickering & Gathercole, 2001). This battery includes three measures of verbal short-term memory (digit recall, word recall and non-word recall), three measures of visuo-spatial short-term memory (block recall, mazes memory, and dot matrix, and three verbal working memory measures (backward digit recall, listening recall, and counting recall) .

Both tests AWMA and WMTB-C provide standardized scores, with a mean value of 100 and a standard deviation of 15, for 4 to 11 year olds (Alloway, 2007; Pickering & Gathercole, 2001).

Intelligence

Intelligence of children with ADHD as a group does not differ appreciably from that of the general population. This is evident from the obtained mean of their IQ scores on *Wechsler Intelligence Scale for Children* third edition (WISC-III) in several studies. The mean of full scale IQ (WSIQ) scores has been found to be 100.9 (Standard deviation or SD=14.8) in MTA Co-operative Group study (1999), 103.83 (SD=12.57) in the study of Kaplan et al. (2000), 107.1 (SD=16.7) in Doyle et al.'s study (2000) and 105.62 (SD=14.43) in the study of Schuck and Crinella (2005). The FSIQ means in all these studies are somewhat higher than that of test standardization population mean of 100 (with SD=15) because children with low IQ or low SES were excluded from the studies, and, except for the

MTA Co-operative Group study (done on 579 children with ADHD) rest of the studies were done on smaller samples (200, 113 and 150 in respective order). The means, after correction, for exclusion of low IQ and low SES children from the studies, might very well be close to the mean of the general population.

Similarly no difference in IQ of children with and without ADHD, was reported in a couple of studies done on very small samples (average 17 to 20) (Mealer et al., 1996; Spivak et al., 1997).

The IQs of children with ADHD are distributed normally. Kaplan et al. (2000) have found that the pattern of intelligence in ADHD children does not differ from the normal distribution, with IQs ranging from below average (lesser proportion), average (larger proportion) to above average (lesser proportion).

The FSIQ scores (derived from WISC-III and estimated from WISC-R norms) ranged from 77 to 135 in 200 children with ADHD, when children with IQs below 75 were removed (Kaplan et al., 2000). The IQs of children with ADHD were speculated to represent the entire spectrum from giftedness to mental disability by Barkley, 1998. Bonafina et al., 2000, found different intelligence scores in the different subgroups of children with ADHD, which emerged after cluster analysis: average, high-average and low scores in intelligence were found in the different subgroups, but very high scores were not found.

Unusually high IQs in children with ADHD as a regular characteristic feature have not been found (e.g. Kaplan et al., 2000) which dispels the notions that these children often are highly intelligent, as suggested by Hallowell and Ratey (1994), or ADHD and giftedness are related (Baum, Olenchak, & Owen, 1998).

Four distinct subgroups of children with ADHD emerged in the cluster analysis study of Bonafina et al. (2000) based on their domains of intelligence. One group was of average intelligence having average abilities in the verbal and non-verbal domains; one group was of average intelligence characterized by relatively strong non-verbal/spatial domains and comparatively weak verbal domains; one group had high scores in intelligence but was moderately low in non-verbal/visuaspatial domains of intelligence; and one group had low scores in intelliegence with considerably lower functioning in both verbal and non-verbal domains. Thus it is seen that children with ADHD differ in their intellectual functiong in different domains of intelligence.

Regarding intellectual functioning in different subtypes of ADHD no clear-cut picture is depicted from the results of studies done so far. Some researchers indicated groups of children with ADHD-hyperactive subtype to have lower verbal IQ than groups of ADHD-inattentive subtype children (Carlson, Lahey, & Neeper, 1986). Other studies found no difference in general intellectual ability in children (eg. Hynd, Lorys et al., 1991; Lahey, Shaughency, Hynd et al., 1987). Similarly in adults also difference in intellectual ability on the basis of ADHD subtype has not been indicated (e.g. Frazier, Demaree & Youngstrom, 2004).

As far as intelligence in ADHD children with learning disabilities is concerned, even its pattern is not different from that of normal distribution. IQs of children with comorbid ADHD and reading disabilities is not lower than IQs of children with only ADHD (Kaplan et al., 2000).

The IQs of children with ADHD are relatively unaffected by their executive function (EF). This has been shown in the study of Reader et al. (1994) on children with ADHD with above average IQ. They found significant deficits in their EF (in relation to normative data) suggesting that significant EF deficits are not necessarily accompanied by lower overall intelligence. The studies of Pennington et al. (1993), Crinella and Yu (2000), and Schuck and Crinella (2005) have shown that general intelligence 'g' and EF are modestly related. This explains the fact that the performance on intelligence tests are relatively unaffected by their deficits in executive function (EF).

Table 2.1 : Cognitive Characteristics of ADHD

Characte-ristics	Description	Reference
Executive function	• Difficulties with planning, organizing tasks and activities, monitoring and checking task performance.	Barkley, (1995); Seidman et al., (2001)
	• Difficulties with goal related behaviours such as establishing goals, holding goals in memory, making persistent efforts towards goals, shaping and redirecting behaviours in order to achieve goals, guidance by inner language, and analysis synthesis of action.	Barkley, (1997a)
	• Problems with : behavioural inhibition the ability to stop or delay responding for periods of time, self-control and self-regulation.	Barkley, (1997b); Sandberg, Day & Trott (1996)
	• Poor sense of time, reduced sensitivity to error, difficulty with simultaneous and sequential tasks.	Barkley, (1998b)
Attention	• Much and most prevalent deficit in domain of sustained attention.	Tsal, Shalev & Mevorach, (2005)
	• Much deficit also in domain of attentional switching/ control.	Preston et al., (2009)

...(Contd.)

Characte-ristics	Description	Reference
	• Less deficit in selective attention.	Preston et al., (2009)
	• Deficit in one domain or in divergent combinations of attentional domains.	Tsal, Shalev & Mevorach, (2005)
Working memory	• Inability to maintain relevant information and ignore or inhibit other information during task.	Van Mourick et al., (2005); Willcutt et al., (2005)
	• Deficit in both verbal and visuospatial domain.	Alloway, Rajendran & Archibald, (2009)
	• More deficit in visuospatial memory than verbal ones.	Martinussen, Hayden, Hogg Johnson & Tannock, (2005)Barkley, (1997);
	• Poorer working memory than normally developing children.	McInnes et al., (2003)
Short term memory	• At par with age expected levels.	Roodenrys, (2006)
Intelligence	• Does not differ much from that of general population.	MTA Co-operative Group, (1999); Kaplan et al., (2000);
	• IQs are distributed normally.	Schuck and Crinella, (2005);
	• Unusually high IQs not found.	Kaplan et al., (2000)

Language and Communication

Children with ADHD have difficulties in language usage (Barkley, 1998a, cited in Lienemann & Reid, 2008). Deficits in language skills mostly involve the use of language to accomplish social action (i.e. the pragmatic function of language) (Jacobson & Kikas, 2007). For example, children with ADHD lack the ability to use self-talk, which is critical for being able to mediate their behaviour and follow prescribed rules (Jacobson & Kikas, 2007); they frequently switch the topic of conversation and their responses are not related to questions asked (Heyer, 1995). These deficits in language skills may cause communication difficulties which may result in social problems. ADHD children with pure inattentive behavior are more likely to have general cognitive delays particularly in the area of language development (Warner-Rogers et al., 2000).

Children with ADHD also lack the ability to keep their thoughts in a logical order, to organize and to categorize linguistic information (Heyer, 1995; Purvis & Tannock, 1997). They are able to comprehend the factual details from televised stories as well as typical children but their performance is poorer in understanding and recalling causal relationships among events in the story (Lorch et al., 2000). Their expressive language is somewhat poorer as compared to control group children (Pisecco, Baker et al., 2001). ADHD children with co-existing reading disability exhibit more impairment in language, particularly worse in receptive language, than children with only ADHD (Pisecco, Baker, Silva, & Brooke, 2001). Children with ADHD-combined subtype and comorbid LD specially have lower verbal abilities (Jacobson & Kikas, 2007). They have difficulties in understanding words which describe relations between objects (e.g. front, back, above, beside) (Jacobson & Kikas, 2007).

Motor Functioning

Motor skills are essential for performing movement tasks. Children with ADHD have difficulties in motor functioning.

This has been shown in the studies of Kooistra et al. (2005), Piek et al. (1999) and many researches on ADHD and movement task performance reviewed by Harvey & Reid, 2003 (cited in Kooistra et al. 2005) Children with ADHD are physically more active (American Psychiatric Association, 1994) but clumsy in motor skills (Piek et al., 1999) and less able to control their motorics (Denckla & Rudel, 1978). They have been found (through regression analysis) to have more fine motor problems than controls (Steger et al., 2001), with less co-ordination in their fine motor tasks than children without disabilities (Barkley, 1997a). Some children with ADHD have also been found to have developmental co-ordination disorder (DCD), a disorder of movement skill acquisition (Piek et al., 1999) . Children with ADHD, are, in general less accurate and more variable in their movements than children with other psycho-pathologies and healthy controls (Kalff et al., 2003). However, motor co-ordination difficulties occur less frequently than deficits in cognitive functioning (Njiokiktjien, 1989). The prevalence rate for motor difficulties in ADHD has been estimated to be close to 50 per cent (Barkley, 1998). It has been found that the gross motor skills and fine motor of children with *ADHD-only* do not differ from those of typically developing children (control), with the exception of visual-motor skills (Kooistra et al., 2005). Visual-motor skill is the ability to reproduce or copy geometric forms, and children with ADHD only were poorer in this than the control group. But Chidren with ADHD with co-occurring reading disability (RD) or oppositional defiant disorder (ODD) or both RD and ODD have been found to have impaired and poorer motor skills (gross, fine and visual-motor skills) than the control group (Kooistra et al., 2005).

Different subgroups of ADHD are possibly characterized by different types of motor problem. Children with predominantly inattentive subtype of ADHD have been reported to be associated with fine motor problems, whereas those with combined subtype of ADHD are likely to be at risk for gross motor problems (Piek et al., 1999; Pitcher et al., 2003). However this association has not been confirmed by the study of Kooistra et al. (2005). More researches are required to study association of different ADHD subtypes with different types of motor impairment.

Factors Associated with Motor Difficulties

The difficulties in motor functioning are possibly due to the co-existing deficits with ADHD. The motor impairment in ADHD has been found to increase as a function of co-existing disorder, the presence of reading disability predicting motor impairment rather than ADHD status (Kooistra et al., 2005). Thus, it is probable motor impairment is not a fundamental part of ADHD (Kooistra et al., 2005).

However it is not yet clear to what extent motor deficits are a primary feature of ADHD and to what extent they may be accounted for by one or more co-existing disorders. Further investigation is needed on this line.

Risk-taking Behaviour

Risk-taking behaviour includes use and abuse of substances such as cigarettes, marijuana, illicit drugs and alcohol, delinquency, act of aggression, dangerous driving and so on.

Substance Use and Abuse

As far as potential association of ADHD with substance use and substance abuse is concerned, it is not yet clear and is debatable. Retrospective studies of adults with substance use disorder have reported high rates of ADHD in them. For example, in a treatment programme for alcohol dependent patients, those with a history of ADHD tended to have an earlier age of onset for alcohol use and dependence than did those without ADHD (Ercan et al., 2003). Longitudinal studies (prospective studies) of children diagnosed with ADHD report more likelihood of these children using or abusing drugs, alcohol or cigarettes in adolescence and adulthood than their respective counterparts without the disorder (Barkley et al., 1990; Milberger et al., 1997; Lambert & Hartsough, 1998; Molina & Pelham, 1999 and Molina & Pelham, 2003).

Various studies have reported more number of cigarettes smoking and episodes of drunkenness in adolescents with ADHD than controls (Molina & Pelham, 2003), more adolescents taking up regular cigarette smoking by age 17 than the age-matched controls (Lambert & Hartsough, 1998) and continued higher rates of daily smoking, dependency on tobacco and cocaine in adulthood than controls (Lambert & Hartsough, 1998).

However, there are also findings from researches which do not show significant differences between ADHD group and non-ADHD group in risk-taking behaviour. For example, Molina and Pelham (2003), reported no differences between adolescents with and without ADHD on alcohol or marijuana use disorder. Lambert and Hartsough (1998) found no relationship between ADHD status and age of initiation to smoking, and also no independent effect of ADHD on risk of problematic substance use was found by Disney et al., 1999.

With regard to ADHD co-existing with learning disability (LD), Molina and Pelham (2001) found only statistically non-significant results for likelihood of engagement in substance use and abuse. But, McNamara et al. (2008), suggested that adolescents with LD and comorbid LD with ADHD may engage in alcohol use, marijuana use and smoking to a greater extent than their peers without any psychological disability (ADHD and LD).

Delinquency

There is a high degree of comorbidity between antisocial behaviours and ADHD (Pisecco, Wristers et al., 2001). Adolescent students with comorbid LD and ADHD are likely to engage more in minor acts of delinquency, sneaking out at night and joyriding than their peers in the control group

(McNamara et al., 2008). The results from the study of McGee, Williams and Silva (1988) have supported the assertion that the presence of early ADHD behaviours would significantly predict the manifestation of later antisocial symptoms.

Aggression

Children with ADHD, particularly those with hyperactivity are likely to exhibit the problem of aggression (Edelbrock et al., 1984), and have been identified as more aggressive towards peers (Lahey et al., 1987). McNamara et al. (2008) found that adolescents with both LD and ADHD are also likely to display more aggressive acts like pushing or shoving someone, swearing, teasing, hitting or kicking someone than the control group peers without psychological disability.

Dangerous Driving

Youngsters with ADHD show less compliance with rules (Pfiffner & Barkley, 1998, cited in Lowe & Reynolds, 2000). They are likely to be engaged in dangerous driving (Jerome & Segal, 1997; cited in Kendall, 2000). In comparison to young drivers without ADHD, youth with ADHD have nearly four times more automobile accidents, are more likely to cause bodily injury in accidents and have three times more citations for speeding (Barkley, 2000b).

Risk Factors for Risk-taking Behaviours

Risk factor indicates a feature or exposure that precedes and is associated with increased risk for a negative behavioural outcome. Variables identified as risk factors do not necessarily cause the negative outcome, i.e., risk-taking behaviour. However, they may mediate or moderate risk.

Various risk factors for risk-taking behaviours have been suggested.

Potential risk factor for substance use and abuse in adolescents with ADHD may be conduct disorder. Studies have reported that most of the adolescents using substances or having substance abuse problems also have conduct disorder (eg. Barkley et al., 1990; Mannuzza et al., 1998; Molina & Pelham, 1999). Molina and Pelham (1999) found that highest rates of problematic alcohol use were among those adolescents with ADHD who also met diagnostic criteria for co-occurring conduct disorder or co-occurring delinquency. Conduct disorder is suggested as a probable risk factor for delinquency also in children and adolescents with ADHD. It has been found in longitudinal studies that children with both ADHD and conduct disorder are likely to have more delinquent behaviour than children with either disorder alone (Loeber et. al., 1990; Moffit, 1990) .

There is some uncertainty regarding learning disability (LD) as a direct or indirect risk for substance use and abuse. Molina and Pelham (2001) found that childhood learning disability (reading and math) among children with ADHD does not predict development of substance use and abuse during adolescence. However, McNamara et al. (2008) reported that it is a combination of LD per se and secondary psycho-social characteristics that is associated with more frequent risk-taking behaviour in adolescents with comorbid LD and ADHD. The four important mediating psycho-social characteristics are: (*i*) the adolescent's relationship with one's mother; (*ii*) the adolescent's engagement in school and extra curricular activities; (*iii*) the adolescent's feeling of well-being; and (*iv*) the adolescent's feeling of being victimized.

Poor academic achievement also appears to contribute to delinquent behaviour among children with ADHD. It has been found in a study that poor academic self-concept predicts antisocial behaviour in early adolescents with ADHD (Pisecco, Wristers, Silva, Swank, & Baker 2001). The academic difficulties or at least the perception of these difficulties may directly contribute to poor academic outcomes and related antisocial behaviour (Preston et. al., 2009).

The level of cognitive functioning has also been suggested as mediator of risk for these children with ADHD. Higher cognitive functioning among such children with ADHD may operate differentially regarding development of sustained tobacco or alcohol usage (Molina & Pelham, 2001). Molina and Pelham (2001) reported that children with ADHD having higher IQs and higher levels of academic achievement in childhood were more likely to try cigarettes, to smoke daily and to have their first drink of alcohol, or first cigarette, at an early age when they become adolescents. In contrast, children with ADHD having better reading achievement were less likely to have later alcohol use disorder.

Deficits in social skills also seem to be associated with substance use disorder. Studies by Greene et al. 1997 and Greene et al., 1999 have found associations between social skills deficits and risk for substance use disorder in individuals with ADHD and their unaffected siblings even after controlling for commonly recognized risk factors.

With regard to pharmacological risks, evidence so far has suggested that stimulant drugs prescribed for ADHD, do not raise the risk for substance use disorder (Biederman et al., 1999) nor does it induce a preference for stimulant drugs (Biederman et al., 1997).

Academic Functioning

ADHD symptoms may contribute to poor performance in academic field. A vast number of studies indicate a negative influence of ADHD on academic achievement as shown by lower scores on standardized tests of achievement ((Purvis & Tannock, 1997, 2000; Lahey et al., 1998; Frazier et al., 2007). However this may not hold true for all individuals with ADHD. There are some studies which suggest that all students with ADHD do not exhibit low academic achievement (eg. Barkley, 1997a; Zentall, 1993; Sparks, Javorsky & Philips, 2004). The findings of Sparks, Javorsky & Philips (2004) study show that all college students with ADHD had successfully passed foreign language courses. The students' classification of ADHD did not interfere with their ability to pass both upper and lower level foreign language courses with average to above-average grades. In fact, there are also some research reports which show higher achievement for individuals with ADHD when compared to controls or to the population expectancy (eg., Abikoff & Gittleman, 1985; Forness, Youpa, Hanna, Cantwell, & Swanson, 1992; Sandson, Bachna, & Morin, 2000). There are evidences to suggest that when IQ is controlled observed difficulties in achievement are markedly reduced in significance in children with ADHD (Willcutt et al., 2001; Willcutt, Doyle, Nigg et al., 2005) and become non-significant in adults with ADHD (Laasonen et al., 2010). Some studies have shown that students may or may not have deficits in a specific academic skill such as reading, spelling or math, depending upon the functiong of intelligence domains (eg. Bonafina et al., 2006). Four distinct subgroups of children with ADHD emerged in the cluster analysis study of Bonafina et al. (2000) based on their domains of intelligence and reading ability. One group was of average intelligence including abilities in the verbal and nonverbal domains and average reading ability; one group was of average intelligence with relatively strong non-verbal/spatial domain and comparatively weak domain but showed impairment in reading ability; one group had high scores in both intelligence and reading, having moderately low non-verbal/visuospatial domain of intelligence; and one group had low scores in both intelligence and reading with considerably lower functioning in verbal and non-verbal domains. Thus, the academic functioning cannot be expected to be exhibited uniformly in all individuals diagnosed with ADHD. Also, the academic difficulties experienced by them at elementary, secondary and post-secondary level of education may be of several kinds.

Children with ADHD are generally at risk for academic under-achievement (Barry, Lyman & Klinger, 2002; Du Paul & Eckert, 1997; 1998, cited in Lienemann & Reid, 2008) and a range of academic complications. They have poorer grades, higher rates of school failure, greater need to repeat years, and are often placed in special education classes, or drop out of school (eg. Barkley, Fischer, Edelbrock & Smallish, 1990; Deshazo, Lyman & Klinger, 2002).

The negative influence of ADHD on academic performance is seen not only in childhood but also in adolescence and early adult life. Different types of academic problems are exhibited. Adolescents with ADHD are likely to have higher rates of school dropouts and suspensions (Hinshaw, 1992; Wilson & Marcotte, 1996). The ADHD youth in college often exhibit problems with study strategies, note taking, summarizing and outlining, and test taking (review by Javorsky & Gussin, 1994; cited in Sparks, Javorsky & Philips, 2004), and they earn lower grades and experience more academic probation in comparison to other students (Heiligenstein et al., 1999). Adults with ADHD are likely to have academic difficulties in reading, spelling and arithmetic (Laasonen et al., 2010; Frazier et al., 2004).

Higher levels of ADHD symptoms are related to lower levels of academic adjustment, poorer study skills, lower career decision making self-efficacy, and lower levels of social adjustment to college (Norvilitis, Sun & Zhang, 2010).

With regard to difficulties in various aspects of academic performance (i.e., speed, accuracy, errors and corrected errors), ADHD adults' difficulties reflect less accurate performance across the domains of reading, spelling and arithmetic (Laasonen et al., 2010). As far as processing speed in adults is concerned there are divergent results. Laasonen and her team (2010) found in one study that adults with ADHD were not impaired in the processing speed variables. Another study by Laasonen and team (2009) reported difficulties in processing speed. Impaired processing speed has been often reported in ADHD (eg. Woods et al., 2002; Shanahan et al., 2006).

The ADHD symptoms have more negative effect on academic achievement in younger age. Thus, children with

ADHD have lower achievement than adolescents with ADHD who in turn, have lower achievement than adults with ADHD (Frazier et al., 2007). Also, different ADHD subtypes can have different learning profiles, academic performance and academic problem (Lämminmäki et al. 1995; Marshall et al., 1997). Children with inattentive behaviour are more likely to have learning problems, poor reading attainment (Warner - Rogers et al. 2000), difficulties in Mathematics (Carlson et al., 1986; Hynd et al, 1991) low self-esteem in school and need instructions to be repeated (Warner - Rogers et al., 2000). College students with inattentive behavioural symptoms are likely to have lower self-efficacy and poorer study skills (Norvilitis, Sun & Zhang, 2010). As attention problems increase, so do academic problems, and vice-versa (Mayes, Calhoun & Crowell, 2000). Symptoms of inattention are associated not only with academic underachievement (Lahey et al., 1998), but also with home work problems, school difficulties (Lahey et al., 1994) reading disability (Willcutt & Pennington, 2000), as well as difficulties in college adjustment (Norvilitis, Sun & Zhang, 2010). Symptoms of inattention seem to be more strongly related to learning problems and academic problems than symptoms of hyperactivity/ impulsivity (Lahey et al., 1998; Lahey & Willcutt, 1998). In fact, when the other dimension was controlled statistically, inattention symptoms were found to be significantly related to academic underachievement in mathematics and reading, but symptoms of hyperactivity-impulsivity were not (Lahey et al., 1998; Willcutt, 1998).

The negative impact of ADHD symptoms is not uniform over all the academic domains. Some children with ADHD have high average skills in reading but are relatively weak in arithmetic and non-verbal skills; others may show relatively strong non-verbal/spatial skills but comparatively weak reading and language related academic skills; and still others may show considerably lower functioning, overall, in the academic areas (Bonafina et al., 2000). In adults, the domain of reading is reported to be most affected followed by maths and spelling (Frazier et al., 2007) whereas another studies suggest somewhat different pattern of academic performance. They suggest that spelling is poorest followed by less impaired arithmetic and reading performance in adults with ADHD (Frazier et al., 2004; Laasonen et al., 2010). This difference in pattern of academic performance is probably due to comorbid learning disability. It has been suggested that when comorbid learning disability is excluded, there is pronounced difficulty in arithmetic and spelling, but less in reading (Frazier et al., 2007; Lassonen et al., 2010). However, there are children with ADHD who have some difficulty with learning even though they do not meet the criteria for learning disability (Mayes, Cahoun & Crowell, 2000). With regard to magnitude of achievement difficulties in different academic domains in ADHD, various researches have suggested medium effect sizes for reading, small to large effect sizes for arithmetic, and medium to large effect sizes for spelling (Bridgett & Walker, 2006; Frazier et al., 2004; Frazier et al., 2007; Hervey et al., 2004; Laasonen et al., 2010).

The academic difficulties in various domains are presented here :

Reading Difficulties

The reading difficulties of individuals with ADHD seem to be in basic reading, that is, decoding of single words, and in reading comprehension. Both speed and accuracy or either of these may be affected in these two areas of reading.

Children with ADHD often perform below average on reading (Olson, 1996). They have impaired word decoding skills as observed frequently in ADHD studies on children (review by Hinshaw, 1992b; cited in Samuelsson, Lundberg, & Herkner, 2004). After controlling for IQ and phonological processing skills, it has been found that children and adolescents with ADHD do not exhibit deficits in reading vocabulary (Nussbaum, Grant, Roman, Poole, & Bigler, 1990) or have problems with the comprehension of short passages (Javorsky, 1996). Instead students with ADHD have difficulties in comprehending longer passages (McGee, Partridge, Williams & Silva, 1991). In adults with ADHD difficulty in word decoding is quite less prevalent in comparison to comprehension reading (Samuelsson, Lundberg, & Harkner, 2004). In fact, no difference was found between adults with and without ADHD on tests emphasizing word decoding (Seidman et al., 1998). Comprehension reading and technical reading have been found to pose difficulty to adults with ADHD (Samuelsson et al., 2004; Laasonen et al., 2010), accuracy in reading is particularly affected which is poorer than the control group for technical reading (Laasonen, Lehtinen, Leppämäki, Tani, & Hokkanen, 2010). Accuracy is also low in comprehension reading in adults with ADHD (Laasonen et al., 2010). After controlling for IQ it has been found that, as in children and adolescents with ADHD, in ADHD adults too, difficulties in reading cease to exist (Laasonen et al., 2010). But, even after controlling for age, socio-economic status, and educational level, ADHD symptoms in adults continue to be significantly associated with reading comprehension difficulties (Samuelsson, Lundberg, & Herkner, 2004).

Within subtypes of ADHD-ADHD-combined subtype and ADHD-inattentive subtype, no difference is there in the two subtype-groups in reading ability as measured using WIAT-II Word Reading (Wechsler Individual Achievement Test-second edition, Wechsler, 2001) (Preston et al., 2009).

ADHD symptoms have a negative impact on reading performance (Frazier et al., 2007). ADHD symptoms interfere more with reading comprehension than with word decoding (Samuelsson et al., 2004). Reading difficulties, particularly reading comprehension difficulties, in individuals with ADHD are possibly due to inattention and executive function deficits "the core features of ADHD, rather than phonological skills deficits (Laasonen et al., 2010). In a study, reading attainment of children with ADHD in the purely inattentive group were found to be lower than that of children in control group (Warner-Rogers et al., 2000). Learning disability as a possible cause for poor reading attainment was ruled out in the study. It has been suggested that deficits in the central executive function may account for reading difficulties (Gathercole & Baddeley, 1993). Indeed, reading comprehension requires controlled allocation of attention, planning, organization, problem-solving and general verbal abilities. This means, reading comprehension involves aspects of executive control and verbal abilities, and thus, may interact to a larger extent with features characterizing ADHD (Samuelsson et al., 2004). As ADHD is a functional impairment in higher level attentional and executive control, one would expect difficulties in comprehension reading.

Word decoding skills are based on linguistic abilities related to speech. This skill is determined by a smoothly operating, encapsulated, and resource-cheap phonological module largely unrelated to higher cognitive functions such as executive controls, planning, constructing, inferencing and organizing (eg., Stanovich & Siegel, 1994). Therefore in adults, symptoms of ADHD do not show strong correlation with word decoding skills (Samuelsson et al., 2004). However, in childhood, the skill of decoding words is under development. Full automatization is not achieved until compulsory school education is completed (Samuelsson et al., 2004). Early reading, including decoding words, is mostly a process under central control. Orthographically complex and lengthy word certainly require attentional resources and working memory (Samuelsson et al., 2004). Therefore, there is more association between ADHD and poor word decoding among children as suggested by Samuelsson et al., 2004.

Phonological skills are less likely to account for reading difficulties in adults with ADHD. This is because phonological awareness, phonological naming and phonological memory in adults with ADHD are not impaired (Laassonen et al.,

2010). This is also confirmed by a study (Samuelsson et al., 2004) in which no differences were obtained in phonological processing skills of adults with and without ADHD. And, if phonological skills are impaired, effect sizes are small to medium (Boonstra et al., 2005; Van Mourik et al., 2005; Hervey et al., 2004). Even in children with ADHD reading difficulties are less likely to be accounted by phonological skills. Normal reading has been observed in children with ADHD who have affected phonological processes in study of Purvis & Tannock, 2000, but not vice versa (Palacios & Semrud-Clikeman 2005; Pennington, Groisser, & Welsh, 1993). Also phonological awareness (awareness of the sound structure of spoken language) is less impaired than phonological naming (and memory) in children with ADHD as suggested by pattern of results in few studies (Felton & Wood, 1989; Hinshaw et al., 2007). Further, phonological processing measures of ADHD-only group have been found to be better than the reading disability-only group (Pennington et al., 1993).

Moreover evidences suggest that difficulties in phonological processing are reduced remarkably in children with ADHD (Willcutt et al., 2001; Willcutt, Doyle, Nigg et al., 2005) and become nonsignificant in adults with ADHD (Laasonen et al., 2010) when intelligence quotient is controlled for. Thus, reading difficulties in ADHD are not or minimally accounted by phonological skills and more by other viriables specific to ADHD.

Writing Difficulties

Children with ADHD have problems with pre-requisite skills for writing, such as, handwriting, taking dictation, or simple transcription of already formulated thoughts and concepts (Hoza & Pelham, 1993; Imhof 2004; Tucha & Lange, 2004; Re, Pedron & Cornoldi, 2007; Kroese et al., 2000). Using language to express thoughts or produce coherent narrative is difficult for them (Purvis & Tannock, 1997; Tannock & Schacher 1996, cited in Lienemann & Reid, 2008).

They experience difficulties in expressive writing in both the qualitative and quantitative parameters (Re, Pedron & Cornoldi, 2007). The *qualitative* parameters include :

(*i*) Adequacy, i.e., adequacy of the written text with respect to the task requirement.

(*ii*) Structure, i.e., organization of the text;

(*iii*) Grammar, i.e, correct use of punctuation, subdivision into paragraphs, correct use of tenses, correct concordance between gender and number of nouns, verbs and adjectives, and use of subordinate clauses.

The *quantitative* parameters include :

(*i*) Length of the text, i.e. total number of words, including articles and function words;

(*ii*) Richness of themes, i.e., number of issues considered;

(*iii*) Percentage of errors (accuracy), i.e., words incorrectly written divided by number of words in the text.

(*iv*) Lexicon, i.e. the quantity and adequacy of the different words used (variety of vocabulary).

The compositions of the children with ADHD are poor in terms of word complexity, written language, productivity and general writing ability (Resta & Eliot, 1994, cited in Lienemann & Reid, 2008). Re, Pedron and Cornoldi (2007) conducted a series of three studies which throw light on the expressive writing skills of children with ADHD. Three groups of ADHD children of different ages were studied alongwith matched controls. The results in all the three studies showed that compared to the control group, children with ADHD, despite having an adequate standard of general abilities, were less proficient in the four qualitative parameters of expressive writing (adequacy, structure, grammar and lexicon). Their text was very simple and poorly organized more similar to a list of elements than to an organized text. The lexicon was poor as they used less number of adjectives and made more repetitions. The subordinate clauses written by them in the text were also low in number showing the poor quality of grammar and syntax. They made more errors and wrote shorter texts (quantitative parameters) than controls. The errors made by them were not due to a general linguistic disability as the ADHD group and control group were matched on this aspect. The series of studies also indicate that ADHD children of all ages, from younger to older age, experience difficulties in writing more than the controls. These studies further indicate that whatever be the type of expressive writing task, whether description task or narrative task, the children with ADHD have the same pattern of writing difficulties.

As far as speed of writing or writing fluency is concerned, it is not a problem in children with ADHD. They have been found to write as rapidly as controls (Ross, Poidevant & Miner, 1995).

Written expression skills is impaired even of those ADHD children who do not have co-existing learning disability (Mayes, Calhoun & Crowell, 2000). The writing skills of ADHD children are poorer than those of typically developing children (Re, Caeran & Cornoldi, 2008). They lag behind even after effective training (Re, Caeran & Cornoldi, 2008). However, they follow the same developmental path of learning stages for other children regarding reading and writing (Re, Pedron & Cornoldi, 2007) as described by Frith, 1985; Tressoldi & Cornoldi, 1991 (cited in Re, Pedron & Conoldi, 2007).

On the basis of ADHD subtypes, in general, similar pattern of performance in expressive writing is seen in the two groups of ADHD children, i.e., children with inattentive and children with combined subtype (Re, Caeran & Cornoldi, 2008) when analyzed through BVSCO (Battery for the Assessment of writing skills of children from 7 to 13 years old, Tressoldi & Cornoldi, 1991). However the inattentive group showed slightly poorer performance.

Spelling Difficulties

Spelling is primarily a phonological orthographic (sound and sound - symbol) task. Spelling may also be, in part, a selective attention task (e.g. Zentall, 1993). Children with ADHD without a specific learning disability, experience difficulties in spelling (MTA Co-operative Group, 1999). They make more spelling errors than other pupils (Frazier et al., 2007; Re, Pedron & Cornoldi, 2007; Re, Caeran & Cornoldi, 2008). After controlling for IQ differences, it has been found that students with ADHD score lower on standardized measures of spelling than their nondisabled (e.g. August & Garfinkel, 1990). The spelling difficulties are possibly due to the fact that the children show poor management of the monitoring and checking processes which is required for spelling accuracy (Re, Pedron & Cornoldi, 2007; Re, Caeran & Cornoldi, 2007). The ADHD children are often impulsive and thus may typically fail to make a systematic revision of the text. Mistakes in spelling may also be due to less capability of ADHD children to pay attention simultaneously to their ideas and to spelling (Re, Pedron & Cornoldi, 2007) or due to difficulties in selective attention (e.g. Zentall, 1993).

Re, Pedron and Cornoldi (2007) observed that the main spelling difficulty encountered by young children with ADHD (8-11 year olds) is not related to severe phonological difficulties (where reading of the written word has a different sound i.e., phonology from the actual word) or lexical difficulties but due to incorrect use of accents (prosody) and intensity of sound (geminates).

When subtypes of ADHD are considered, no difference is found in children with combined subtype and inattentive subtype in their spelling ability on WIAT-II (Wechsler Individual Achievement Test-Second edition, 2001) spelling test (Preston et. al., 2009).

Handwriting Difficulties

Children with ADHD exhibit handwriting difficulties in addition to specific problems with one academic area such as reading, spelling or math, or along with overall problems in academics. The handwriting difficulties of children with ADHD may be due to visual-motor deficits (Zentall, 1993). When controlling for visual-motor skill, differences in handwriting errors between students having ADHD and non-ADHD students were not significant (Zentall & Kruczek, 1988). This finding of Zentall and Kruczek suggested that handwriting difficulties could be the result of deficits in visual-motor skill. Alternatively, both poor handwriting and deficits in visual-motor skill may be the result of a third variable"failure to sustain attention to tasks that involve repeated practice (Zentall, 1993). Zental and Kruczek (1988) found that students with ADHD made more errors and had poor handwriting ratings on a copying task than non-ADHD students even after repeated practice on the task.

Arithmetic Difficulties

Children with ADHD perform poorly on computing in math—both speed and accuracy are affected (Zentall, Smith, Lee & Wieczorek, 1994). Studies have shown that on timed tasks of math calculation, children with ADHD performed significantly lower than their peers without ADHD, even when differences in IQ were controlled (Ackerman, Anhalt, Holcomb, & Dykman, 1986; Zentall, 1990; Zentall, Smith, Lee & Wieczorek, 1994). These children exhibit error patterns in arithmetic (Benedotto Nasho & Tannock, 1999) which affects accuracy in the subject. They commit rounding mistakes and fail to carry integers on simple math problems (Frazier et al., 2007).

It has been speculated that the slower speed of students with ADHD on math tasks might be attributed to their inability for sustained attention on repetitive task, difficulty in retrieval from memory and lack of mastery of rote skills. It has also been suggested that students with ADHD may have more difficulty on timed math tasks because of a combination of weaker computational skills, slower visual-motor speed, and more off-task behaviours (Barkley, Anastopoulas,

Guevremont, & Fletcher, 1991; Zentall, 1990). Disruption in the ability to retrieve basic arithmetic facts from long-term memory may result in poor performance of children with ADHD in timed tasks of calculation (Zentall, 1990). This disruption in retrieval process in ADHD children perhaps may be due to working memory difficulties in inhibiting the retrieval of irrelevant associations, as discovered by Barrouillet et al., (1997) and confirmed by Geary et al., (2000) in students with learning disabilities. Gross-Tsur et al., (1996) suggested inhibitory mechanisms to be potential contributors to the co-occurrence of ADHD and arithmetic disability in some children. Another feature, automatization, required for speed in arithmetic is affected in children with ADHD (Ackerman et al., 1986). Basic arithmetic facts need to be overlearned and memorized until automatized for rapid calculation. Problems of retrieval from memory and memorization to the point of automaticity have been identified as some of the reasons underlying arithmetic difficulties by Elkins (2002; cited in van Kraayenoord & Elkins, 2004). There is evidence from literature that deficits in the central executive, such as poor attentional control, disrupts the execution of arithmetic procedures (Hitch, 1978; McLean & Hitch, 1999). The procedural errors committed while solving more complex, multistep arithmetic problems, like errors while carrying or borrowing from one column to the next, may be due to difficulties in monitoring and co-ordinating the sequence of problem solving steps, which in turn indicate the involvement of the central executive (Geary, 2004). Central executive deficits are common in ADHD.

Based on subtypes of ADHD, there is no difference in numerical operations of two groups of children, i.e., in ADHD-combined and ADHD-inattentive subtype as measured on WIAT-II Numerical Operations (Wechsler, 2001) (Preston et al., 2009).

Like children with ADHD, adults with ADHD have difficulties with accuracy and make errors (Laasonen,

Lehtinen, Leppamaki, Tani & Hokkanen, 2010). Their arithmetic accuracy has been found to be poorer than the control group (Laasonen, Lehtinen, Leppämäki, Tani & Hokkanen, 2010).

It has been suggested that performance of adults is less accurate due to difficulties in attention and executive functions. The difficulties in components of these areas, such as difficulties in response inhibition vigilance, spatial working memory, and planning could easily lead to lowered level of accuracy (Laasonen et al., 2010) in arithmetic.

Table 2.2 : Academic Functioning

Area	Characteristics	Reference
Reading	• Children often perform below average in reading measures.	Olson, (1996)
	• Word decoding skills is often impaired in children.	Review by Hinshaw (1992)
	• Both children & adults have difficulties in comprehension reading.	McGee et al. (1991). Samuelsson, Lund-Berg, & Herkner (2004)
	• Reading accuracy in adults is poorer than the control group.	Laasonen et al., (2010)
	• There is no difference in reading ability in children with combined and inattentive subtypes of ADHD.	Preston et al., (2009)
Writing (Expre-ssive)	• Children have difficulties in qualitative parameters (which include adequacy, structure, grammar) as well as in quantitative parameters (which include length of the text, richness of themes, percentage of errors, and lexicon).	Re, Pedron & Cornoldi, (2007)

...(Contd.)

Area	Characteristics	Reference
	• There is similar pattern of performance in expressive writing in children with combined and inattentive subtypes.	Re, Caeran & Cornoldi, (2008)
	• Speed of writing is not a problem for them, they write as fast as controls.	Ross, Poidevant & Miner (1995)
Spelling	• Children and adults with ADHD have difficulties in spelling, and make more errors than other students.	MTA Co-operative Group (1999); Frazier et al., (2007); Re, Caeran & Cornoldi, (2008)
	• There is no difference in children with combined and inattentive subtypes in their spelling ability.	Preston et al., (2009)
Hand-writing	• Children with ADHD have difficulties in handwriting. • Students with ADHD make more errors and have poorer handwriting in copying task than non-ADHD students.	Zentall & Kruczek (1988) Zentall & Kruczek (1988)
Arithmetic	• Children and adults with ADHD have problems in computing.	Zentall, Smith Lee & Wiezorek (1994);
	• Both have difficulties with accuracy.	Laasonen et al. (2010);
	• Children have slower speed than their peers without ADHD.	Ackerman et al., (1986)
	• Automatization required for speed is affected in children with ADHD.	Ackerman et al., (1986)
	• There is no difference in numerical operations in children with combined and inattentive subtypes.	Preston et al., (2009)

Causes of Academic under Achievement in ADHD Children

In children, adolescents and youth with ADHD, the factors associated with underachievement in academic areas are: (*i*) specific ADHD related behaviours; (*ii*) specific cognitive deficits; and (*iii*) external factors, as revealed in recent studies.

Specific ADHD Related Behaviours

The poor academic achievement of students with ADHD, particularly children is linked to specific ADHD related behaviours like leaving seat frequently, looking away and excessive talking in the classroom. A study by Zentall, Smith, Lee and Weiczorek (1994, cited in Preston et al., 2009) reported that children with ADHD performed more poorly on math computations because they were slower and less accurate than controls, in addition to exhibiting more off task behaviours; children with ADHD were more frequently out of their seat, looking away and talking more than controls, which could clearly impact speed and accuracy of performance.

Specific Cognitive Deficits

Besides observed ADHD related behaviours, some other studies have pointed out with the help of neuropsychological testing, specific cognitive deficits in ADHD to contribute to poor academic performance. Children with ADHD who have cognitive functioning deficits are more likely to have academic problems than children with ADHD who do not have cognitive functioning deficits (Biederman, Monuteaux & Doyle, 2004). Academic tasks requiring revision, present problems for children and students with ADHD, as they require attention to detail and redoing a task (Zentall, 2005; cited in Lienamann & Reid, 2008) Merrell and Tymms (2001) reported that a teacher rating of inattention as in DSM-IV (Diagnostic and Statistical Manual of Mental Disorders-Fourth Edition; American Psychiatric Association, 1994) was significantly higher in children who performed poorly on achievement tests of reading and math. The specific deficits in sustained attention and attentional control/switching contribute significantly to academic difficulties. There is a small but significant relationship between sustained attention and academic performance in children with ADHD, as found by Aylward, Gordon and Verhulst (1997). Sustained attention predicts variance only in math and probably in other academic areas. The domain of selective attention does not account for variance in any achievement domain as revealed in the study of Preston et al. (2009) but it may play a larger role in classroom settings (Preston et al., 2009). Attentional control/ switching, which involves and utilizes components of executive cognitive functions of inhibition, working memory and set shifting accounts for academic underachievement in all areas (reading, math and spelling) in children with ADHD (Preston et al. 2009). The deficit in attentional control/ switching plays more important role in impaired academic performance than any other attention domain (Preston et al., 2009).

Therefore, some of the academic difficulties experienced by children with ADHD are due to deficits in attention, executive functions, working memory rather than the presence of a specific learning disability per se. Inability to sustain attention, and to adequately inhibit and shift attention, impaired temporal processing, deficits in working memory and in other executive functions like planning, organizing, goal setting, monitoring, response inhibition and vigilance, are linked to poor academic functioning in ADHD children. All these can easily lead to lowered level of accuracy in general, and in the domains of reading, spelling and arithmetic in particular, in adults too (Laasonen et al., 2010).

External Factors

Apart from these ADHD related symptoms and cognitive deficits, external factors are also thought to be responsible for academic underachievement. External factors such as difficult academic environment at a particular college or university, loss of family structure that supported academic success, and absence of individual education services, as probable causes of academic underachievement have been hypothesized for college students with ADHD. This hypothesis resulted from a study conducted on students with ADHD studying in college by Heiligenstein et al. (1999). They found that majority of the participants did not have academic problems that were apparent during childhood. So they proposed that the onset of academic impairment may be related more to external factors than to ADHD symptoms per se.

Hence, it is of utmost importance to understand the pattern and development of academic impairment in ADHD to provide adequate services and support in education, mental health, and other areas of concern.

SUMMARY

The various characteristics features are not uniformly displayed, they are displayed differently in different individuals with ADHD. The characteristics described are cognitive functioning, language and communication, motor functioning, risk taking behaviour, and academic functioning. The major cognitive characteristic of ADHD is impaired executive system. The executive system is primarily responsible for co-ordinating activity within the cognitive system and the amount of information that can be held in the memory storage systems. Examples of executive function deficits are difficulties with planning, organizing tasks, monitoring and checking task performance, difficulties with attentional switching/control, working memory tasks, and problems in goal-related behaviours. Cognitive deficits in attentional function are another important features of ADHD. Attention is a complex, multidimensional concept comprising of three domains of sustained attention, selective attention and attentional switching/control. Children with ADHD exhibit a variety of attention problems reflecting deficits in various attention domains. Different children with ADHD manifest divergent combinations of attention deficits. ADHD is characterized by deficits in working memory. It is the ability to store and manipulate information for brief periods. Intelligence in ADHD population is more or less similar to the general population barring very high intelligence which is not typical of ADHD. Difficulties in language usage and motor functioning are seen in children with ADHD. ADHD symptoms may contribute to risk-taking behaviour and poor academic functioning, but this may not hold true for all individuals with ADHD. Impaired academic functioning is seen in the form of reading, writing, spelling and arithmetic difficulties. The ADHD symptoms have more negative effect on academic achievement in younger age, and do not have uniform influence over all the academic domains. Also different ADHD subtypes can have different learning profiles, academic performance and academic problem.

CHAPTER 3

Causes

There is no compelling evidence as yet which pinpoints a single cause of ADHD. Rather, several factors seem to give rise to the condition. These are:

- Genetics
- Brain dysfunction
- Environment

Genetics

Studies indicate that there is influence of genetic factors on ADHD. Studies done on family, adoption and twins over the past three decades have convincingly demonstrated the familial basis of ADHD. For 81 per cent of the identical (monozygotic) twins genetics contributed to the disorder as compared to only 29 per cent for non-identical (dizygotic) twins (Gilger et al., 1992). ADHD occurs more often in biological relatives of those with the disorder than would be expected in the general population. The percentage of close relatives in the families of children with ADHD who have ADHD is 25 per cent in comparison to about 5 per cent in the general population (Biederman et al., 1990). Retrospective studies have shown that approximately 25 per cent of the natural parents of children with ADHD, compared with 4 per cent of adoptive parents, had histories of ADHD (Deutsch, 1987).

There is a greater risk of ADHD for siblings of a person with ADHD, especially when parents have a history of ADHD, and monozygotic twins are more likely to be concordant than dizygotic twins (McMahon, 1980). The genetic contribution to the disorder is greater when the symptoms are more serious. The evidence supports contribution of genetics, which has yet to be completely identified. Molecular genetic studies have focussed on dopamine transporter and dopamine receptor (D4) genes with ADHD (e.g. Cook et al., 1995; Lattoste et al., 1996; Swanson, Sunohara et al., 1998; Swanson, et al., 2000). It has been shown by Swanson, et al. that a particular polymorphism in the dopamine receptor D4 (D4R4) gene located on chromosome 11 p 15.5, is associated with blunted sensitivity of the D4 receptor, which is prominently found in brain regions that play a role in attention (eg. anterior cingulate gyrus). There is considerable research work on genes that control other aspects of dopamine system, which include the dopamine receptor D2 gene DRD2, (Comings et al., 1991); the dopamine transporter gene, DAT1 (Gill, Daly, Heron, Hawi, & Fitzgerald, 1997); and the dopamine β-hydroxylase gene, DBH (Kuperman, Kramer, & Loney, 1988), not to mention genes related to other neuro-transmitter systems. Hence, symptoms of ADHD will be manifested by children due to accumulation of polygenic influences that evoke behaviours which are diagnosed as ADHD behaviours.

Brain Dysfunction

One early theory was that brain damage led to ADHD. But researchers often could not find a link between brain damage and ADHD. In studies of identified cases of ADHD, only 5-10 per cent were found to have brain damage in the past, and most children with well documented brain damage did not develop ADHD (Rutter, 1977).

However, studies have suggested that impaired brain functioning may be the cause of ADHD. Children with ADHD perform poorly in tasks requiring vigilance and impulse restraint (e.g. Homatidis & Konstantareas, 1981) and other tasks sensitive to brain function (e.g. August, 1987; Douglas, 1983). Scientists in recent studies have focused on the functions of different parts of the brain, to search the cause of ADHD. Different parts of the brain have been studied through the use of various methods for seeing into the brain, or imaging the brain. Besides this, functioning of specific parts of the brain have been studied through neuro-psychological tests of different kinds. Studies on the brain of ADHD children and non-ADHD matched controls have linked psychological deficits in ADHD children to their brain. In earlier days when data from brain imaging and genetic studies were not available, frontal lobe dysfunction was presumed to be the neural basis for ADHD. It was Fletcher (1996) who admonished that it was wrong to ascribe executive functions (which is dysfunctional in children with ADHD) to the frontal lobes. Evidences obtained from neuro-anatomical and neuro-psychological studies converge on the finding that the EF system includes the frontal cortex and interconnected subcortical structures.

Study of Posner & Raichle (1994) has demonstrated that the anatomical network that apparently subserves EF is located in the anterior cingulate gyri, left lateral frontal lobe and basal ganglia. Recent brain imaging studies of children with ADHD have identified dysmorphologies in these and anatomically contiguous neural structures. Atypical brain morphology have been reported in basal ganglia (Aylward et al., 1996), right fronto-striatal circuitary (Casey et al., 1997), and caudate nucleus (Castellanos et al., 1994; Hynd et al., 1993). The neural structures that are involved in EF system are located in the brain's dopaminergic pathways, in particular the mesolimbic and nigrostriatal dopaminergic systems (Schuck & Crinella, 2005). Most studies have reported anatomical differences between children with ADHD and controls that involve the nigrostriatal or frontostriatal networks and closely interconnected structures (eg. Denckla & Reiss, 1997), that can be termed the EF system (Schuck & Crinella, 2005).

Some studies have found that the ADHD children as a group had 3-4 percent smaller brain volumes in all regions—the frontal lobes, temporal gray matter, caudate nucleus and cerebellum than the matched control group children without ADHD (Castellanos *et al.*, 2002).

Animal studies have also been done to identify discreet brain areas that might have linkage with EF. Studies conducted on rodent EF system have found that bilateral lesions to any one of eight subcortical structures (substantia nigra, caudatoputamen, ventral tegmentum, pontine reticular formation, globus pallidus, ventro-lateral thalamus, median raphe, and superior colliculus) significantly affected performance on a wide variety of problem solving tasks (Crinella & Yu, 2000; Thompson, Crinella, & Yu, 1990 cited in Schuck & Crinella, 2005). These subcortical structures mediate executive function (EF) components such as: (1) shifting cognitive sets (Thompson, 1982a, 1982b; Thompson & Yang, 1982); (2) response flexibility (Thompson, Harmon & Yu, 1984); (3) response inhibition (Thompson, Bjelajac, Huestis, Crinella & Yu, 1989); (4) transfer strategies (Thompson, Bjelajac, Fukui, et al., 1989); and (5) working memory (Thompson, Huestis, Bjelajac, Crinella, & Yu, 1989). Study on laboratory rat has shown that the EF system must be intact for performing adequately on a wide variety of laboratory problem solving tasks (Crinella & Yu, 2000).

Clinical observations of children with ADHD also seem to suggest involvement of Basal ganglia in EF. Evidence obtained from brain imaging in these clinical studies have demonstrated that basal ganglia structures are at least as probable as the prefrontal cortex as cause of ADHD (Denckla

& Reiss, 1997). Similarly, the correlative neuroanatomical evidence demonstrated basal ganglia involvement in EF (Folstein, Brandt, & Folstein, 1990; Middleton & Strick, 1994., Philips & Carr, 1987; cited in Schuck & Crinella, 2005). The basal ganglia are the interconnected gray masses deep in the cerebral hemisphere that connect the cerebrum and the cerebellum.

Environment

Various environmental factors have been associated with a higher risk of ADHD.

Studies have shown a possible correlation between the use of cigarettes and alcohol during pregnancy and risk for ADHD in the baby to be born.

Lead used in wall paints may be another factor responsible for ADHD. Exposure to toxic levels of lead may put young preschool children at risk.

Social environment is correlated with ADHD, particularly the child's failure to learn adequate cognitive and behavioural skills. It contributes to shaping of ADHD behaviours (O'Leary,1980). There are several social factors which can contribute to a child's failure to acquire sufficient self-control. These are : (*i*) a lack of a structured learning environment; (*ii*) observing others' inappropriate behaviour; (*iii*) receiving rewards for fast guessing, (*iv*) not being taught cognitive strategies for focusing attention; and (*v*) disruption and disorganization in the home (Kendall, 2000). For example, dysfunctional parent-child interactions seem to result in a variety of childhood problems (Wahler & Dumas, 1989). However, there are few studies which have examined the social environment as a cause of ADHD. Children with ADHD receive more direct commands and supervision from their parents than other children, but these actions of parents seem to be result rather than the cause of the ADHD behaviour. Environmental factors seem to be less responsible for initiating

ADHD, and play a more important role in the course and ultimate outcome of ADHD (Braswell & Bloomquist, 1991).

It had been suggested that consumption of large quantities of refined sugar can cause hyperactivity or aggravate symptoms of ADHD. However, a more recent study on the effect of sugar on children, showed no significant effects of the sugar on behaviour or learning (Wolraich, Milich, Stumbo, Schultz, 1985). Similarly eating foods containing preservatives and artificial colours was thought to be cause of ADHD but is not supported by evidence. Claims were made in the early to mid 1970s that a change in diet could reduce hyperactivity (Feingold, 1975). But rigorous tests undertaken by scientists generally failed to support the hypothesis that diet or diet modifications, could have a significant impact on ADHD (Conners, 1980). In fact, the more rigorous the investigation, the less support it provided for the diet hypothesis (Swanson & Kinsbourne, 1980). Therefore a person's diet as a possible cause of ADHD lacks sufficient evidence and may be ruled out.

SUMMARY

There is no compelling evidence as yet which pin-points a single cause of ADHD. Rather, several factors seem to give rise to the condition. These are genetics, brain dysfunction and environment. Studies done on family, adoption and twins have demonstrated the familial basis of ADHD. ADHD occurs more often in biological relatives of those with the disorder than would be expected in the general population. Molecular genetic studies have pointed to polygenic influences that evoke ADHD behaviours. Impaired brain functioning is suggested to be another cause of ADHD. Scientists in recent studies have focussed on the functions of different parts of the brain, to search the cause of ADHD. Some studies have found that the ADHD children as a group had 3-4 per cent smaller brain volumes in several regions than the matched conrol group children without ADHD. Frontal cortex and subcortical structures including basal gandia have been also pointed out for ADHD-like functioning. Various enviornmental factors have been associated with a higher risk of ADHD. Cigarette smoking, alcohol use by expecting mothers, social environment and exposure to toxic elements seem to play a role in the course and outcome of ADHD.

CHAPTER 4

Identification and Assessment

Presence of ADHD is not simple to identify. Not everyone who is overly inattentive, or extremely impulsive or excessively active has ADHD. Most people sometimes blurt out things they mean to say, or switch from one task to another, or become disorganized and forgetful. This does not mean they all have the problem of ADHD.

Conditions necessary for identification are :

- The essential behavioural features of inattention and/or impulsivity-hyperactivity must be demonstrated to a degree that is inappropriate for the individual's age.
- The behaviours must appear early in life before age seven and continue for at least six months.
- Above all, the behaviours must become handicapping in at least two settings of life such as in the school, on the playground, at home, in the community or in other social settings.

So, someone who shows some of the symptoms but whose learning in school or relationship with peers or parents are not impaired by these bahaviours would not be diagnosed as an ADHD individual. Similarly, a child who seems hyperactive on the playground but functions well elsewhere cannot be considered as an ADHD child. Therefore the behaviours need to be observed across situations–at school, at home and in social settings–before the presence of ADHD can be declared.

The critical questions considered to detect ADHD in a child are thus :

- Are the behaviours of inattention, impulsivity and/or hyperactivity excessive ?
- Do the behaviours occur more often than in other children the same age ?
- Have the behaviours been occurring for the last six months?
- Did they appear early in life, before age seven ?
- Are the behaviours a continuous problem, not just a response to a temporary situation ?
- Do they occur in several settings or only in one specific place like the playground or in the school?

Thereafter the child's pattern of behaviours is compared against a set of criteria and characteristics of the disorder as listed in the DSM-IV-TR, mentioned earlier.

Several separate assessments are made for identifying ADHD in children. No single test has been devised that definitely diagnoses ADHD in a child (Gordon & Barkley, 1998). Parents and teachers should be included in this. Signs of inattention, hyperactivity and impulsivity in the child are seen by some parents early in life long before the child enters school. The child's loss of interest in playing a game or watching a TV show, or his/her running around in home completely out of control may be noticed by the parents.

Sometimes the teacher is the first to recognize that a child is hyperactive or inattentive when unnoticed by parents. Since teachers work with many children they come to know how 'average' children behave in classroom and other school settings where attention and self control are required.

Ideally the diagnosis should be made by a professional. If ADHD is suspected by parents or teachers they should turn to specialists in the field for diagnosis. Sometimes, it so happens, that parents and teachers fail to notice the signs of ADHD in children who may be more inattentive and passive yet who are quiet and co-operative, such as those with the predominantly inattentive form of ADHD. In such situations professionals can diagnose the disorder. Professionals should also routinely screen students for ADHD symptomatology at post-secondary stage too (Frazier, Youngstrom, Glutting & Watkins, 2007). The professionals who can help in this may be the child psychiatrists and child psychologists, developmental/behavioural paediatricians, clinicians counselors or behavioural neurologists who are most often trained in differential diagnosis.

To identify ADHD the first task of the specialist is to gather information that will rule out other possible reasons for the child's behaviour. Among possible reasons for behaviour like that of ADHD are the following :

- A sudden change in the child's life—the death of a parent or grandparent; parents' divorce; a parent's job loss
- Undetected seizures, such as in petit mal or temporal lobel seizures
- Medical disorders that may affect brain functioning
- Underachievement caused by learning disability
- Anxiety or depression.

Several separate assessments are involved in identifying ADHD in children. These are studying records of the child, parents' and teachers' ratings, interviews with the child, parents and teachers, direct observation of child's behaviour and task performance, psychological testing and medical examination of the child.

Studying Records of the Child

The child's school and medical records are checked. A school record of hearing or vision problems may be available for studying if maintained in schools. A specialist tries to determine whether the home and classroom environment are unusually stressful or chaotic, and how the child's parents and teachers deal with the child. Checking of records helps in ruling out other possible causes of ADHD like behaviour.

Parents' and Teachers' Ratings and Other Measures of the Child's Behaviour

The child's parents, and present as well as past teachers are asked to rate their observations of the child's behaviour on standardized evaluation forms, known as behaviour rating scales. The child's behaviour is then compared to that of other children the same age. While rating scales might seem very subjective, teachers often get to know so many children that their judgement of how a child compares to others is usually a reliable and valid measure. Checklists for child's behaviour can be used to place the level of the child's problem in comparison with other children. Various parent rating forms are available in the western countries, such as the *Conners Rating scales* (Conners, 1990); *Conners Parents Rating Scales-Revised,* (Long Version) (CPRS-R:L; Conners, Parker, Sitarenios, & Epstein, 1998), Corners Parent Rating Scale (CPRS-R, Conners, Sitarenios, Parker & Epstein, 1998a) and the *ADHD rating scale-IV* : Home version and School version (DuPaul, Power, Anastopoulos, & Reid, 1998). Rating scale forms for specifically obtaining teacher ratings are also available for example, Conners Teacher Rating Scale (CTRS-R, Conners, Sitarenios, Parker & Epstein, 1998b).

Barkley and Edwards (1998) recommend the use of two kinds of rating scales, the broad band rating scale and narrow bond rating scales, and also additional scales depending upon the child's dimensions of child psychopathology. Some examples of these scales are *Behaviour Assessment System for*

Children-Parent Rating Scale, Teacher Rating Scale, and Self-Report of Personality (BASC; Reynolds & Kamphaus, 1994) and the *Child Behavior Checklist*—Parent Report Form (Achenbach & Edelbrock, 1983), Teacher Report Form (Achenback & Edelbrock, 1986a), a Youth Self-Report (Achenback & Edelbrock, 1986b). Narrow band scales are used to assess specific symptoms of ADHD. Examples of these scales are the *Disruptive Behaviour Rating Scale* (Barkley & Murphy, 1998). To assess other specific areas of concern for example, peer relations or adaptive functioning some additional rating scales of behaviour may be included.

There are other parent measures for identifying ADHD symptoms in college going students. One such measure is *College ADHD Response Evaluation* (CARE; Glutting, Sheslow, & Adams, 2002, cited in Frazier et al., 2007). The CARE can be used for double purpose: (*i*) screening; and (*ii*) as a part of comprehensive ADHD assessment depending upon the examiner's background and training. Disability service providers who are not well qualified and trained use it for screening purpose to identify college students who are at risk for having ADHD. Examiners with appropriate training use it for comprehensive assessment of ADHD (Frazier et al., 2007). CARE comprises of two measures: *Student Response Inventory* (SRI, a self-rating scale) and Parent Response Inventory (PRI). The PRI is an objective rating scale completed by a college student's parent. It contains items on the ADHD criteria as does the SRI. An assessment of ADHD that relies only on self-report of students runs the risks of under—or over report of clinically important phenomena. This is due to the difficulties of inattention, poor concentration and behavioural dysregulation encountered by ADHD student. So the PRI was developed to supplement the data supplied by students on the SRI.

Parents and teachers may differ in rating the different ADHD constructs. Parents are better at rating one ADHD construct—the inattention trait (Burns et al., 2003; Konold &

Glutting, 2008) whereas teacher better rate another ADHD construct—the hyperactivity impulsivity trait (Konold & Glutting, 2008). Clinicians diagnosing ADHD should pay more attention to results from the inattention trait when parents are the raters, and to results from the hyperactivity-impulsivity trait when teachers are the raters. The ratings from both parents and teacher can make valid assessments of ADHD.

Interviews with the Child, Parents and Teachers

Interviews are held with the child, parents, teachers and other people who know the child well, such as other family members, coaches or baby-sitters. Clinical interview conducted with the child is helpful in the assessment of ADHD. The content of the interview is decided according to the age of the child. For a preschool child, the interview is a means of establishing rapport and noting the appearance, behaviour, developmental characteristics, and general demeanor of the child. For a school age child or adolescent the interview is aimed to gather information about the child's or adolescent's views on the reason for the referral evaluation and difficulties encountered (Barkley & Edwards, 1998). Parents and Teachers are asked to describe the child's behaviour in a variety of situations. The details of the child's behaviour or social context that may not be obtained from rating scales can be had through interviews. Interviews with parents and teachers can be particularly helpful in assessing whether the child's behaviour is consistent across different situations and what conditions enhance or reduce the problematic behaviours. For instance, the presence of certain teachers, or classmates or a certain classroom seating arrangement may be associated with a worsening of symptoms of an ADHD child in the classroom (Kendall, 2000). Thus, the interviews conducted with the parents and teachers yield highly descriptive information about the child and the child's psychological adjustment at home and at school.

Direct Observation of Child's Behaviour and Task Performance

Valuable information can be gathered by observing the child in class and other settings for assessment of ADHD. For example, trained specialists can differentiate between hyperactive and nonhyperactive children by observing and recording bahaviour—such as out of seat activity and disruptiveness (eg,. Milich, Loney & Roberts, 1986).

To observe task performance the child is given match-to-sample problem. In this, a standard picture is shown above six others, only one of which matches the standard (eg. Matching Familiar Figures Test; Kagan, 1966). The child's task is to find the one of the six pictures that matches the standard picture at the top. Responses of the child in matching the picture are observed and found to be useful in identifying hyperactive children (Homatidis & Konstantareas, 1981). ADHD children's reaction to this problem is impulsive behaviour—rushing to guess, without looking carefully at the alternatives. They show short latencies to respond and a high rate of errors, (Kendall, 2000).

Psychological Testing of the Child

Parents and teachers of children with ADHD may be unaware of the exact extent of the academic delay in them. This holds true particularly for parents and teachers of children with ADHD with inattentive subtype (Warner-Rogers et al., 2000). Formal evaluation of cognitive and academic functioning using standardized and valid psychometric measures provide a more powerful and valid estimate of their abilities than simple parent or teacher reports. Also, standardized tests of intelligence and learning achievement tests are administrated to find out if the child has a learning disability and whether the disability is in one or more subjects. In most cases, the child is assessed for social adjustment and mental health.

According to Gordon and Barkley (1998), the psychological tests to evaluate ADHD fall into four categories:

(1) intelligence/achievement measures; (2) neuropsycho-logical batteries (e.g., Luria-Nebraska Neuropsychological Battery, Halstead-Reitan Neuropsychological Test Battery); (3) individual neuropsychological tests; and (4) projective/personality measures.

The neuropsychological tests aid diagnosis and treatment (by identifying adaptive capacities, strengths, and limitations) and are also used to assess change over time (Seidman, 1997). If the question about learning disability in a child with ADHD arises, a comprehensive assessment of cognitive and academic skills is essential (Dewey, Kaplan, Crawford, & Fischer, 1998).

Medical Examination of the Child

A complete medical examination is imperative to determine that a child has ADHD. The medical interview and the physical examination constitute the medical examination of the child. The medical interview focuses on differential diagnosis, evaluates possible co-existing medical conditions and determines if any physical conditions exist that may prevent the use of medicines for treatment of a child with ADHD. The physical examination includes numerous screening tests, a neurological examination, and a neuro developmental examination (Barkley & Edwards, 1998).

The results of these various sources of information are studied in detail. Specialist pays special attention to the child's behaviour during situations that are the most demanding of self-control, for example, classroom, as well as noisy or unstructured situations such as parties, recess in school, or during tasks that require sustained attention, for example, reading, working on mathematics problems or playing a board game like carom, ludo. A profile of the child's behaviour is then prepared by putting together information from varied sources. Certain questions are put forth : Which ADHD like behaviours listed in the most recent DSM does the child show? How often? In what situations? How long has the child been doing them ? How old was the child when the problem started? Are the behaviour problems relatively chronic or enduring or are they periodic in nature? Are the behaviours seriously interfering with the child's friendships, school activities, home life, or participation in community activities? Does the child have any other related problems? The answers to these questions help identify whether the child's hyperactivity, impulsivity, and inattention are significant and long standing. If so, the child may be diagnosed with ADHD.

A combination of assessment techniques are generally employed to determine if the child meets the criteria needed for a diagnosis. The early and accurate identification of children with ADHD is critical to ensuring that children receive services that will help them to be successful academically, socially and in other aspects of life. A consensus among professionals, advocacy groups and researchers is needed regarding the identification and implementation of improved procedures for ADHD identification.

SUMMARY

Presence of ADHD is not simple to identify. Not everyone who is overly, inattentive, or extremely impulsive or overactive has ADHD. Conditions necessary for identification are that the essential behavioural features must be demonstrated to a degree that is inappropriate for the individual's age, the behaviours must appear early in life, and the behaviours must become handicapping in at least two settings of life. Several separate assessments are made for identifying ADHD in children. These are studying records of the child, parents' and teachers' ratings, interviews with the child, parents and teachers, direct observation of child's behaviour, psychological testing and medical examination of the child. The results of these various sources of information are studied in detail for diagnosing ADHD.

CHAPTER 5

Interventions

Several intervention approaches are there for ADHD. But no single intervention or treatment is the answer for every child with ADHD. Sometimes a combination of these are required depending upon the child's needs and personal history. The efforts of parents, professionals and school teachers are included and integrated for better and effective results.

Currently the foremost interventions for ADHD are:

- Medicinal Intervention
- Psycho-social interventions
- Educational interventions
- Multi-model intervention

Medicinal Intervention

Medications have been used for years to treat the symptoms of ADHD. Stimulants are typically used in medication for ADHD and seem to be effective. Some of the psycho-stimulants prescribed are Ritalin and Concerta (methylphenidate), Dexedrine and Dextrostat (dextroamphetamines), Adderall (amphetamine), Focalin (dexmethylphenidate) and Cylert (pemoline, causes side effects affecting liver).

Methylphenidate and dexamfetamine are recommended as first-line pharmacological intervention by various health organizations funded by their governments (National Institute for Health and Clinical Excellence 2008, cited in Akram et al., 2009). Barkley et al., (1991) reported that treatment with methylphenidate led to improvements in the behaviour of children with ADD/H or ADD/WO, as assessed by rating scales.

The effects of psychostimulant medication on symptoms of ADHD can be immediate and dramatic (Greenhill, 1998). These psychostimulants which affect multiple neuro-transmitter systems, have powerful effect on attention and activity levels. They can reduce the hyperactivity and impulsiveness of children with ADHD and can increase their ability to focus attention, work and learn. Treatment with stimulant medication alone is usually found to have a positive benefit for children with ADHD (MTA Cooperative Group, 1999) particularly in improving EF (executive functioning) (Barnett et al., 2001; Douglas et al., 1988; Whalen & Henker, 1991 a). For example, Schwean et al. (1993) showed that specific cognitive processes, e.g., planning, attention, simultaneous and sequential processing, in other word EF, are indeed sensitive to stimulant. Barnett et al. (2001) too showed that medicated children with ADHD scored higher than non-medicated children with ADHD on spatial working memory, considered to be an EF-saturated task. Pharmacological intervention is believed to enhance the child's ability to use intellectual resources by optimizing EF (Schuck & Crinella, 2005). The medications may also improve physical coordination as needed in sports and performance on fine motor tasks such as that needed in handwriting (Spencer et al., 1996). In addition, medications (Ritalin) have been found to reduce the intensity of anger in children with ADHD without altering the content of the children's response (Hinshaw, Henker & Whalen, 1984a, b).

Some children get better results from one medication, some from another. Also, different dozes are appropriate for different ADHD subtypes as the pharmacological agents may show differential effects in the different ADHD subtypes. Study of Barkley et al. (1991) indicated, after behavioural observation and performance on psychometric tests, that for children with ADD/WO (ADD without hyperactivity) low dozes of methylphenidate led to optimal improvements whereas, higher dozes were needed for optimal improvements in for children with ADD/H. It is important that right medication and proper dose must be given with medical supervision keeping in mind the level of activity and inattention in these children.

The stimulant medications also have potential, unwanted side effects. The most common side effects are insomnia, increased anxiety, irritability, low mood/sadness, weight loss, increased blood pressure and heart rate, and occasional motor tics (Barkley, McMurray, Edelbrock, & Robbins, 1990), decreased appetite, stomach problems, dizziness and headaches. Decreased appetite and headache are relatively more common side effects (Akram et al., 2009). Also, these medications cannot be given to all children with ADHD, neither do all children on these medications show any improvement (Whalen and Henker, 1991a). Moreover, the effects of the drugs are not long-lasting, persisting only till they are taken in the majority of these children who show improvement (Kendall, 2000). Therefore medications should not be overused and given as a quick-fix measure for ADHD behaviours.

Medications do not cure ADHD, they only control the symptoms temporarily. Although these medications help the child pay better attention and complete school task, they cannot increase knowledge or improve academic skills and classroom performance. They help the child to use those skills he or she already possesses.

Psycho-social Interventions

O'Leary (1980) once said that hyperactive children need skills, not just pills. Psychosocial interventions employ behavioural and cognitive behavioural techniques to teach children the skills necessary to pay attention, engage in self-control, and reduce or better modulate excessive motor activity. These techniques include modifying the environment and providing structured opportunities for children to learn the self-control skill that they can apply in new situations (Kendall, 2000).

Psycho-social intervention characteristically include behaviour management, structured classroom management programmes, and training in social and cognitive skills. Generally, psycho-social interventions are carried on with the support of parents and teachers in schools, who are trained by therapists.

The psycho-social interventions do not produce immediate effects as they are not fast acting. Also, their effects may be somewhat less apparent. But, they have the potential for persistence over time. This is generally concluded from the observation that the skills, were actually learned through psycho-social techniques and continued to be applied elsewhere (Kendall, 2000).

Parent training and educational interventions are dealt separately here though they are mostly based on psycho-social intervention.

Behaviour Management

Behavioural approach is applied to handle disruptive behaviours and promote change. It includes the techniques of :

1. Rewards and penalties
2. Shaping of behaviour

3. Immediate feedback
4. Structuring situations

1. Rewards and penalties: This technique involves rewarding the ADHD child's good behaviour or work and punishing the misbehaviour immediately.

A small reward is given for performing desirable behaviour such as asking for a toy or waiting for turn, and mild penalty for not doing so or inappropriate behaviour like grabbing a toy, or not completing a simple task. Reward can be given in the form of token or point systems. A token can be exchanged for special privileges the ADHD child wants and is eager to earn. For example, it can be a cookie or toy liked by the child or a game or any activity the child enjoys doing. The penalty might be taking away the token or a brief time-out i.e stopping from the activities liked by the child, or isolation to a chair or room. When the child becomes too unruly or out of control, time-outs are used in which the child is removed from the agitating situation and sits alone quietly for a short time to calm down. Penalty or punishment should not be harsh or excessive because then, it can cause serious inhibitions. A child who is punished very frequently may become too much withdrawn, aggressive, unwilling to do anything and potentially depressed. The goal, eventually, is to help children learn to control their own behaviour and to choose the more desirable behaviour. This technique of rewards and penalties is effective for modifying children's behaviour; although children with ADHD may need more frequent rewards.

2. Shaping of behaviour: The principle of operant conditioning of Skinner (1953) is applied in this. The desired behaviours are strengthened and the disturbing behaviours are weakened. This is done gradually in successive small steps. Thus the entire desirable behaviour need not be produced at a time by the ADHD child to receive reinforcement. Rather, closer and closer approximations of desired response are rewarded until gradually a new step is mastered by the child, and then reinforcement is shifted and provided only after this new step.

3. Immediate feedback: Feedback means telling the child about his action or behaviour whether it is appropriate or inappropriate after it has been displayed. This knowledge about behaviour is given immediately after its occurrence. The good actions or behaviour and the negative ones too, when noticed are promptly pointed out to the child. Praise or reprimand may also be given alongwith feedback depending upon the appropriateness of the behaviour. But sometimes less serious, unwanted actions may be ignored, and reprimand or punishment used sparingly. Children with ADHD often receive and expect criticism. Good behaviour in the ADHD child should be looked for and praised.

4. Structuring situations: It involves organizing situations in such a manner that allows maximum accomplishment for an ADHD child. It includes providing a learning situation with least distraction. Conditions that overstimulate the child are removed or minimized. It has been shown in the study of Schuck & Crinella (2005) that highly structured environment of testing laboratory (reduced distractions, high interest stimuli) enable the children with ADHD to solve complex problems. Thus, setting a daily schedule, arranging room, work place or any other setting in order, dividing a complex task into smaller subtasks and providing greater supervision and encouragement in relatively tedious situations allow maximum a complishment for ADHD child.

The less structured enviornment at school increases the risk of performance deterioration of ADHD child (Schuck & Crinella, 2005). Therefore, the ADHD child's desk should be moved closer to the teacher and away from distractors like windows and doors. Toys, new objects or any other attention drawing things should be kept away from the child's view to minimize distraction while studying or working. The ADHD child should be given any one toy or plaything at a time, or only one or two playmates may be allowed at a time to avoid overstimulation.

Children with ADHD have difficulties in organizing activities. So, a schedule for daily activities should be prepared which is followed everyday from wake-up time to bedtime. The day-to-day routine should include time for homework, play and recreation activities. The schedule should be easily noticeable, it can be pasted in front of the ADHD child's bed or on the almirah door. If a change in schedule is necessary, it should be done in advance as far as possible.

All things should be arranged and kept in order with a definite place for everything. This means, clothings, books, schoolbags, and playthings should all be kept in their proper places for easy functioning of the ADHD child.

Children and teenagers with ADHD need consistent, and straightforward rules that they can understand and follow. They should be helped to know the reasons for each rule. For example, if a daily schedule is set, it should be made clear to the ADHD child or teenager why the schedule is set or why some particular activity is to be done at certain hours only; or if a specific space is fixed for keeping things, why it is so. It helps to have charts showing rules—for home, school and social circles. Daily schedule and household tasks can also be displayed on charts with space to check off what is done.

Social Skills Training

This training helps ADHD children learn new behaviours needed in developing and maintaining social relationships, such as, waiting for a turn, sharing toys, asking for help, or responding to teasing. In social skills training, the appropriate behaviours are first discussed, with the children, followed by modelling or demonstration by experts/therapists which is observed, and then practiced by children. Social skills acquired through training enables the child to develop better ways to play and work with other children.

Cognitive Skills Training

Cognitive skills training helps ADHD children learn skills of focussing attention, problem-solving and self-control such as self-evaluation and self-reward. This training also helps in improving working memory of children with ADHD (Klinberg et al., 2005). For example, the ADHD children are helped in self-monitoring their own behaviour, giving self-praise for acting in a desired way such as controlling anger or thinking before acting. Cognitive-behavioural strategy is used in training of these skills (eg. Hinshaw & Erhardt, 1991; cited in Kendall, 2000). This strategy combines the direct efforts to teach the cognitive skills and behaviour management procedures. Thus, it employs behavioural performance-based procedures, modelling and rewards in training of cognitive skills such as focussing attention and solving problems. One of the goals of the cognitive-behavioural strategy is shaping and encouraging the child to internalize the skills learnt in behaviour management programme and applying these in situations other than that in which it was learnt (Kendall, 2000). It strives to instill the skills which can last and continue across settings, but only a few research reports have shown generalization of one aspect of ADHD (impulsivity) (Kendall, 2000). The goal of generalization outside and after the programme has not always been achieved (Abikoff, 1991).

In their studies, Hinshaw, Henker and Whalen (1984a,b) provided and compared a cognitive-behavioural programme and medication (Ritalin) for anger control in children with ADHD. Relative to the children's behaviour before treatment, the behaviour after treatment was less fidgety and verbally less aggressive in all conditions. The ADHD children receiving the cognitive behavioural treatment had higher ratings of self-control and displayed more appropriate coping behaviours than the children receiving just medication. Unfortunately the researchers did not undertake follow-ups to determine whether the bebeficial gains were temporary or long lasting.

Educational Intervention

The aim of educational intervention is to enable the child with ADHD to gain maximally from classroom instruction and other teaching learning situations in school and/or home. For developing educational intervention plans, a knowledge of a child's cognitive profile, behavioural profile and ADHD symptomatology is necessary. As the ADHD child grows up, he/she should be routinely assessed particularly at post secondary stage by clinicians and counsellors (Frazier et al., 2007). A picture of his or her strengths and weaknesses is valuable in overall planning of interventions, understanding and stimulating the academic performance of the child. School professionals should collaborate and consult with the school psychologists and counsellors regarding programmes and strategies of intervention for ADHD children. The child's educational needs, symptoms of ADHD should be assessed, cognitive and behavioural profile prepared, intervention strategies designed and then implemented to increase the child's achievement in academic and non-academic endeavours. In view of their diverse cognitive and behavioural profiles, the different subgroups of ADHD children may require distinct psychological and educational intervention. Primary intervention, for ADHD children having deficits in verbal and language abilities, should aim at verbally mediated deficits and weaknesses in language related academic skills. On the other hand, ADHD children with severe behavioural difficulties and possibly non-verbal learning deficits would more likely benefit from an array of behavioural intervention targeting their deficits in inhibitory control and social emotional functioning. Furthermore, cognitive interventions may be helpful for remediation of visual-spatial difficulties of other ADHD children with these difficulties. Working memory overload and consequent task failure can be prevented by strategies which break down tasks into smaller components, make complex information simple for remembering and use long-term memory to assist recall

(Gathercole & Alloway, 2008). Children with ADHD can benefit from such strategies.

The findings that learning disabilities and ADHD are separate disorders (eg. Monuteaux et al., 2005; Faraone et al., 1993; Gilger et al., 1992; O'Neill & Douglas, 1991; Lahey et al., 1988) which frequently co-occur, have important implications for intervention. Considering that both ADHD and learning disabilities (such as dyslexia, dyscalculia) have significant associated academic dysfunction, children with both disorders are at higher risk for academic failure. Whereas ADHD can be treated pharmacologically or with behavioural, or cognitive behavioural strategies, learning disabilities require academic remediation (Monuteaux et al.,2005). The diagnosis and treatment of children with ADHD presenting learning disabilities requires a comprehensive approach, encompassing both psychiatric and psychological components. The psycho-social intervention strategies such as behavioural and cognitive behavioural strategies are applied in educational settings. The educational setting may be classroom or other teaching-learning situation in school or at home.

School

Classroom management programmes are in use in which the teachers first determine academic and behavioural goals and reinforcers for each child. The child's behaviour in the classroom is then rated daily on a checklist prepared for this purpose. According to the results of the checklist at the end of the day or at the end of the week, the child could receive reinforcers (O'Leary, Pelham, Rosenbaum, & Price, 1976). This classroom management programme is effective while it is operating, but diminishes in effectiveness after it is discontinued (Kendall, 2000).

Technique of behaviour modification is useful in classroom situation with ADHD children. The teacher administers positive consequences, i.e., reinforcements (e.g., praise or token) and negative consequences i.e., punishments (eg., reprimands and time-out) immediately after the behaviour, with more positive consequences than negative consequences. This seems to be very effective with ADHD children (Pfiffner & Barkley, 1998).

As it is currently stressed that ADHD is the result of a deficit in self-regulation (Barkley, 1997a, 1998a), cognitive-behavioural strategies are also used with ADHD children. Self-control and self-management are emphasized in these cognitive-behavioural strategies. These strategies include goal setting, self-instruction, self-reinforcement or reward, self monitoring and problem solving, that focus on cognitive control. The cognitive-behavioural strategies may yield less positive results according to DuPaul & Stoner, 1994. But according to Lienemann and Reid, 2008; and Reid et al., 2005, these show pronounced positive effect. One such strategy, self-regulated strategy-development (SRSD) model was used in combination with a writing strategy, to enhance writing skills of ADHD children. The effects were positive on writing stories (Lienemann, Graham, Leader-Janssen & Reid, 2006) and essays (Lienemann & Reid, 2008).

Another strategy used in schools is peer tutoring in which the child with ADHD is taught by other students of the class or the classmates. Peer tutoring is found to be effective with ADHD children in improving classroom behaviour and academic performances (DuPaul & Henningson, 1993). These peer tutoring strategies appear to have more positive effects when children with ADHD are paired with well-balanced and conscientious students (Pfiffner & Barkley, 1998).

Regardless of the specific strategy used, there are some general principles which appear to be useful to counteract inattention, hyperactivity, and impulsivity found in ADHD children (Children with Attention Deficit Disorder, 1992 cited in Yesseldyke & Algozzine, 2006).

For Inattention

1. ***Reducing the length of the task:*** A large task is divided into smaller parts when two tasks are to be done, the

less preferred task is completed first, before the more preferred one.

2. *Making tasks interesting:* One of the ways is allowing work with partners in small groups. Another is to make the ADHD child sit closer to the teacher.
3. *Increasing the novelty of the task:* This is especially important for tasks to be done in the later periods of school and tasks that are lengthy. This can be achieved by changing the setting or by employing novel ways to do a task.

For Hyperactivity

1. *Channelling excessive activity:* Excessive activity is channelled into acceptable avenues without attempting to reduce it. The incessant movement of the ADHD child is not inhibited but used in other activities gainfully. The child is actively engaged in purposeful activities to promote learning.
2. *Using activities as rewards:* The good work or behaviour of the ADHD child are rewarded by giving some tasks to do. For example, the ADHD child is allowed to clean the black board, organize teacher's desk or arrange chairs in the class.
3. *Using active responses in instruction:* The ADHD child is encouraged to respond actively during the process of teaching. For example, the child responds by talking, moving or working at the blackboard. Instructional processes which incorporate active responding, are used in classroom teaching. Daily writing, reading, drawing, painting are also encouraged.

For Impulsivity

1. *Substitute responses while waiting:* The child with ADHD is given substitute verbal or motor responses to make while waiting for his/her turn.

2. ***Stressing Note-taking:*** Taking down notes in the classroom, noting home-work to be done in diaries, are stressed for the ADHD child.

Home

Parents or other family members are involved in intervention at home. Parents generally with their own nurturing experience and awareness of their child's unique features, and, understanding of the nature of their child's difficulties may come up with their ingenuous ways or strategies to assist their child with learning of behaviour, skills, facts and concepts at home, and thereby foster his/her development. Nonetheless there are training programmes which equip the parents for managing their child's behaviour and improving academic performance.

Parents learn about basics of ADHD and how to manage their child's behaviour using various tools and techniques (example Anastopoulos, 1996; Braswell, 1991). They learn the skills to reduce their child's non-compliance and develop his/her self-control. Parents are taught behaviour management skills to use with their child. They learn to reward appropriate behaviour, shape desired responses, reduce and eliminate inappropriate behaviours, and use additional rewards to maintain behaviour gains. Use of a brief 'time-out' from desired activities can be an effective punishment for misbehaviour. Parents may also be taught to give the child 'quality time' each day in which they share a pleasurable or relaxing activity. During this time together, the parent looks for opportunities to notice and point out what the child does well, and praise his or her strengths and abilities.

In addition, parents learn to structure situations in ways that will allow their child to succeed. This may include allowing only one or two playmates at a time, so that their child doesn't get overstimulated. Or if their child has trouble in finishing tasks, they may learn to help the child divide a large task into small steps, then praise the child as he/she completes each step.

Parents should also be assisted to develop views about learning difficulties which focus on support for student's improvement, such as the teaching of strategies for learning and the importance of encouragement efforts (van Kraayenwood & Elkins, 2004). They also need to be helped to acquire knowledge and skills about when and how to intervene (van Kraayenwood & Elkins, 2004).

Parents also get to learn stress management through methods of meditation, relaxation techniques and exercise. This increases their own tolerance and they can respond more calmly to their child's disruptive and inappropriate behaviour.

Parent training programmes have been found to reduce the stress of parents and produce overall improvements in their children's ADHD symptoms (Anastopoulos, Shelton, DuPaul, & Gouvremont, 1993).

Home School Collaboration

Collaboration between home and school is one more way to produce effective results. Parents and teachers identify a few desirable behaviours that they want to encourage in the child and strive to instill those behaviours in the children making joint efforts. In this way a continuity is maintained in what the child learns in school and at home. The advantage of home-school collaboration is that it addresses the behaviour across a variety of settings such as home, school and social situations. This increases the probability of generalization and maintenance of the desired behaviour (s). Partnership between parents and teachers is also imporant with respect to tackling learning difficulties of children. Children's academic success is greater (as a consequence of instructional support and intervention) when there is parental involvement, and they tend to regress when there is paucity or lack of parental support (Nichols, 2000). This home school collaboration is also helpful to teachers because it is less labour intensive for them (Kelly, 1990).

Academic Intervention

It is seen that a variety of interventions have been introduced to help ADHD children. The majority of the educational interventions have focused on reducing the frequency of disruptive behaviour and other behavioural symptoms displayed by children with ADHD (DuPaul & Eckert, 1998) or counteracting the ADHD behaviours. The intervention programmes that include academic intervention are few in number (Re, Caeran & Cornoldi, 2008). Some academic intervention programmes designed and developed have yielded optimistic results with ADHD children. They have been helpful in improving the academic performance of ADHD children. Academic intervention for writing is described hereafter.

Academic Intervention for Writing

Writing is not simply transcription of thoughts, ideas and concepts, rather it is a complex process. It requires the involvement of a high degree of complex cognitive procedures besides pre-requisite skills.

1. *Pre-requisite skills:* These comprise of graphic and orthographic skills, as found with dictation, transcription and spelling skills.
2. *Cognitive (functions)/processes:* A series of executive cognitive processes are involved in the task of executive writing. These are working memory, planning, ideas or content generation, translation of ideas into written language, organization of composition, attention to the composing process, monitoring and revising (Graham & Harris, 2003; Burnett & Kastman, 1997; Hayes & Flower, 1980).

Children with ADHD experience difficulties with all aspects of the writing process, whether they are the prerequisite writing tasks of handwriting, spelling and transcription (Imhof, 2004; Tucha & Lange, 2004; Kroese et al., 2000; Re, Pedron & Cornoldi, 2007) or procedures of higher order writing, i.e., using language for verbal description, producing coherent narratives or expressive thoughts (Resta & Eliot, 1994; Re, Pedron & Cornoldi, 2007; Re, Caeran & Cornoldi, 2008).

Some intervention procedures have been developed to improve expressive writing of ADHD children. They have yielded positive outcomes in children with ADHD.

The intervention procedures for improving expressive writing can be divided into two categories based on the approaches employed. These are :

I. Intervention procedures using specific and full-strategy approach.

II. Intervention procedures using a more general approach.

I. Intervention procedures using specific and full strategy instructions approach

These procedures include explicit and systematic teaching of a series of task-specific strategies. These strategies help the student to accomplish an academic task or problem (eg. opinion essay writing). Such an approach involves sustained, direct and systematic instruction designed to facilitate student mastery (Graham & Perin, 2007, cited in Re, Caeran & Cornoldi, 2008) of skills, processes or knowledge. It includes *explicit strategies for planning*, revising and/or editing text; and *writing strategy*, i.e., specific instructions for grammar, sentence combining, and generating essay elements (Re, Caeran & Cornoldi, 2008).

One such approach to intervention procedure is Self-Regulated Strategy Development (SRSD) model developed by Harris & Graham, 1996, cited in Lienemann & Reid, 2008; and Graham & Harris, 1989.

(*i*) In SRSD instruction students are enabled in self-regulation by teaching how to set goals, monitor their own performance and how to use self-instructions, and/or self-reinforcement.

(*ii*) Emphasis is laid on independent use of the writing strategy by the students and accompanying self-regulation procedures. Students learn when, where and how to apply these procedures.

(*iii*) Responsibility for self-regulation procedures gradually shifts from the instructor to the students.

(*iv*) Individualized instructional support and feedback are given so that they are responsive to every child's needs. Students proceed from one instructional stage to another at their own pace.

(*v*) Instruction is not time-based but criterion-based. So students move to later stages of instruction only. When they have met the criteria for doing so.

The SRSD model comprises of two strategies :

A. Planning strategy (POW)

B. Opinion writing strategy (TREE)

A. Planning strategy (POW) : This is a general planning strategy used to frame the writing process. It comprises of three steps for planning and writing. It teaches students to use TREE for composing their opinion essays. The steps involved in the planning strategy (POW) are :

- *The first step* of POW is to *pick an idea* to write about (an opinion essay, for example). Choosing an idea or topic helps the students in planning their compositions, essays, stories, narrowing their focus, and thus they begin to formulate their thoughts.
- *The second step* of POW is to *organize* notes and ideas into a comprehensive writing plan by using TREE.
- *The final step* of POW is to *write and say more*. Students write their essays in this step, using their writing plan and add to it as they write their composition.

B. Opinion Writing Strategy (TREE) : It is a genre specific strategy to guide students' composition of opinion essays. It includes a series of four self-directional prompts. These prompts are used to guide the students about the basic elements of an essay. The steps involved in TREE are as follows :

- *The first step* is *topic sentence.* The topic sentence makes clear about the author's opinion. Students learn what a topic sentence is in this step.
- *The second step* of TREE is to *provide reasons*. Three or more reasons are to be provided by students to support their opinion.
- *The third step* is to *give examples*. To support their reasons examples have to be given by students. They are prompted to question themselves "why do I believe this?"
- *The final step* of TREE is the *ending* in which students learn to write a concluding statement. The final or concluding statement enables the reader to know that the essay or story is complete.

Implementation of SRSD

The strategies involved in SRSD model are implemented in several stages :

1. In the *first stage* of instruction, background knowledge is developed. Students are introduced to the two strategies-POW and TREE. POW is introduced first followed by TREE strategy. Students are given a graphic organizer with picture of tree to assist them in remembering the parts of TREE.
2. In the *second stage* of instruction, there is discussion on the two strategies. Students are instructed to continue the focus on the importance and uses of the two strategies. They are required to remember the steps of the strategy. ADHD student practices to find essay elements and analyze own opinion essays.

In this stage student is also taught goal setting and self-monitoring the number of essay elements he/she includes in his/her opinion essays.

3. In the *third stage* of instruction, the process of using the POW and TREE strategies are explicitly modelled by the instructor by focusing on self-instruction and self-talk. Then, the instructor, collaboratedly with the student, generates an opinion essay including all the elements of essay writing. As ideas are produced, the instructor records the responses on the planning sheet while using the strategy, a variety of self-statements are used by the instructor : For example, "what is my goal?" (goal setting) "what is my next step?" (planning), "does that make sense?" (self-evaluation), "I like that part" (self-reinforcement), and "I am almost done" (coping).

   After the essay is written, the instructor and the student identify all elements in TREE and also count the number of words written.

4. The *fourth stage* (support-stage) is a collaborative writing experience. The instructor and the students together write opinion essays using POW, TREE and a graphic organizer. This stage is student controlled, the instructor providing support only when necessary. Instructor support fades as the student becomes more proficient with the strategy. The student writes the essay based on the notes generated. After the essay is written, the student identifies each part of TREE. Then the student determines if he or she has met his or her goal.

5. The *final stage* is the stage of independent performance. This is reached when student is successfully able to write an opinion essay (including all the parts of TREE) independently without any assisstance.

Advantages/Positive points of SRSD Model (Lienemann & Reid, 2008)

1. The SRSD model directly addresses the ADHD problem of establishing goals, holding goals in memory, persisting in efforts towards goal completion, and shaping and directing behaviours in order to achieve goals.
2. It explicitly develops self-regulation (e.g., self-monitoring) through strategies that improve ability to maintain focus and effort in ADHD children (Reid, Trout & Schartz, 2005).
3. The problem of working memory deficit in children with ADHD is also addressed by this model. Demand or working memory is reduced by the SRSD instruction. This is done by presenting instruction is small steps, teaching strategies to achieve automaticity and providing systematic scaffodded practice (Dawson & Guare, 2004). In addition, prompts, cues, and organizers are provided initially to support efforts. This lessens the burden on working memory and allows students to focus on the task at hand" performing the strategy.

The SRSD model has been found to be effective in improving expressive and narrative writing of ADHD children. The positive effect on performance (opinion essay writing) was maintained after 4 weeks (De La Paz, 2001), the opinion essays written by them were longer, more complete and of better quality (Lienemann & Reid, 2008) and the narrative compositions (stories) too were longer, more complete and qualitatively better (Lienemann, Graham, Leader-Janssen & Reid, 2006).

II. Intervention procedures using a more general approach

This approach given by Re, Caeran & Cornoldi, 2008, provides procedural facilitation. It is a more general approach to scaffolding of students writing it involves providing some form of assistance that helps the child carry out one or more processes required in the writing task (Graham & Perin, 2007, cited in Rae, Caeran & Cornoldi, 2008). The assistance is in the form of guide scheme which facilitates expressive writing. The guide scheme is to be followed by the children while writing essay or letters.

The Guide Scheme

The guide scheme consists of a series of boxes in which the children are asked to record their initial ideas. In this scheme the writing process is broken down into a series of steps. At each step a box is there in which children have to write their ideas. The first box is for the introductory part, e.g. beginning of the essay or letter, then several boxes for the main body, e.g. five boxes for five ideas on the topic, an additional box for other associated ideas, and lastly, a final box for the conclusion (See figure No.).

Prior to using the guide scheme, training is imparted to children with ADHD to help them use the facilitation—the guide scheme.

The Training

The duration of the training is of one hour. During this session the trainer (a psychologist) and children do the writing task (eg. letter writing) together using the guide scheme. In this way children get familiarized with the facilitation (guide scheme) and understand the support. They practice writing with the help of the guide scheme.

The training session for expressive writing consists of the following steps :

1. *Discussion of the task of writing* (for eg. a letter), the trainer at the very beginning asks the children, "Do you find it difficult to write a letter?" and so forth.
2. *Distribution of the guide scheme :* The trainer distributes the guide scheme to the children. Thereafter he/she

introduces the guide scheme by reading it to the children.

3. *Filling the guide scheme* (with trainers assistance) : The trainer asks some of the children to read the matter (eg. letter) they had written the week before. Thereafter trainer asks questions by following the guide scheme, "How did you begin the letter?" then "What is the first thing you wrote? And the next thing?" "Some other ideas?" and so on. The most frequently written sentences are written on the blackboard and the children copy them into the guide scheme.
4. *Introduction of the new task* : In this step the trainer introduces a new task (writing a new letter) to the students who are by now familiar with the facilitation: "Your new task is to write another letter, but this time you should use the guide scheme you were just shown. Any questions?" "Anything that you have to ask?"

During the training session prompts are given to children. These prompts are designed to be interesting and unbiased with regard to gender or socio-economic status.

The guide scheme is useful and gives effective facilitation only when children are trained to use it, otherwise, children produce poorer texts, and make more errors than the controls (Re & Cornoldi, 2007). Thus scaffolding procedure (facilitation through guide scheme) can be effective only if children recognize its importance and are trained to use it.

It has been found that the expressive writing skills of ADHD children improved through the help of a guide scheme preceded by brief training (Re, Caeran & Cornoldi, 2008). The improvements were seen in the following parameters : 1. Reduced spelling errors; 2. More text length; and 3. More ideas/themes generated. More importantly, this intervention procedure can be used with positive effect within the classroom on a large group of children with ADHD symptoms and no other evident symptoms (Re, Caeran & Cornoldi, 2008).

The Guide Scheme

Underline (using a red pen) the main topic of the letter, as described in the title. In the title underline the addressee of the letter. Now develop your letter following the instructions below and write your ideas in the empty boxes.

Describe how you plan to start your letter.

Now write all your ideas for topics of your letter. Write each idea in a separate box.

Reread what you have written. Try to develop one of your ideas in the following box. You can add some details to make your letter more interesting.

How do you plan to conclude your letter?

Multimodel Treatment

It is a combination of different interventions or therapies to bring desirable effects on ADHD. It may involve the integration of medication with behaviour management techniques or cognitive training programmes and/or with academic intervention. Since any intervention in isolation is not very effective with ADHD children, as shown by the researches till date (Bradley & DuPaul, 1997), long term combination treatments have been used. Findings of studies generally indicate that the combination of stimulant medications with behavioural or cognitive therapy can be successful with ADHD children (eg. MTA Co-operative group, 1999) and more efficacious than medications alone (Rapport *et al.*, 1993), or intensive behavioural training programmes (MTA Co-operative Group, 1999)

One advantage of combined treatments for ADHD children is that lower doses of medicines can be effective than medication alone treatment (MTA Co-operative Group, 1999). Again, in some areas like anxiety, academic performance, parent child relations and social skills, combined treatment is superior to medication alone or behaviour therapy alone (MTA Co-operative Group, 1999). As far as persistence of effects of combination treatments is concerned, their examination shows that, barring some inconsistencies, they (effects) have potential to last over time. The effects persist over time to the extent that the skills taught in the therapy were actually learned and applied continuously.

However, more researches are needed before accepting the growing belief that the combination of medication and behavioural, or cognitive-behavioural training may offer the most comprehensive treatment for ADHD children.

Teacher Preparation for ADHD

Many of the symptoms of ADHD are evident in the classroom (Cooper & O' Regan, 2001). School teachers are frequently faced with the difficult task of containing ADHD behaviours. They use a variety of strategies and techniques to contain ADHD behaviours (Cooper & Bilton, 2002; cited in Akram et al., 2009). School teachers, especially special teachers, have an important role to play in the management of the disorder, understanding the need of the students with the disorder, and providing adequate intervention, support and services in time. For this, they should have a sound knowledge about the disorder and its treatment (Akram et al., 2009). Its effective treatment often requires a multimodal approach encompassing pharmacological, behavioural/ psychological and educational interventions.

Teachers often lack knowledge of the basic facts, concepts and understanding about ADHD, and they also tend to believe or endorse some of the myths associated with ADHD (Jerome, Gordon, & Hustler, 1994; Barbaresi & Olsen, 1998; Scuitto, Terjesen, & BenderFrank, 2000; Bekle, 2004; Kos, Richdale, & Jackson, 2004; West et al., 2005; cited in Akram et al., 2009). Even special teachers do not have better knowledge about ADHD than general teachers (Snider, Busch, & Arrowwood, 2003). Many teachers frequently tend to regard the disorder as simply a part of disruptive behaviour in general which lasts till childhood (Akram et al., 2009).

They often may also have false belief that ADHD is caused or can be modified through dietary changes (Akram et al., 2009). They are often unaware that psychostimulant medications (the first choice in pharmacotherapy) is prescribed and given for ADHD symptoms. The effects of these psychostimulants on ADHD symptoms can be immediate and dramatic (Greenhill, 1998), so teachers need to distinguish the two situations—one, when medication has been taken, and the other, when it has been not taken (Akram et al., 2009). These medications can have side effects too, awareness about these could be helpful to the teacher as the child's behaviour or functioning in the classroom may be affected by the side effects. A child may feel dizzy, irritability, or sadness in the classroom due to the side effects of these medications.

Further, the field of special education has a strong research base that special teachers need to use in their daily professional work (Billingsley, 2004). Several intervention measures including instructional strategies have been devised and developed by researchers particularly, for students with ADHD symptoms, most of which can be employed in the classroom situation. Awareness about these strategies could be of immense help for school teachers. Not only this, various types of instructional accommodations for ADHD symptoms have also been listed by the researchers. Some of these are distraction free instructional environment, regular meeting with instructor or teacher, appropriate seating arrangement-preferably near the teacher, extended time for tests, ample time to study tests, and alternative test format. Awareness of these accomodations could help the teachers in effective transaction of classroom activities and also its proper management. This in turn can enhance the academic performance of students with ADHD. Every student is different and unique in himself/herself. So, accomodations, and instruction must be student centred and authentic (Reid & Valle, 2004) . Accordingly, a teacher should be a responsive curriculum planner and informed decision maker. He/she should be teaching to students' strengths rather than their deficits (Reid & Valle, 2004). These are the effective practices which yield positive results.

However, best practices are rarely known, much less implemented by special teachers, who are not adequately prepared to work with the students with disabilities (Rosenberg, 1996). Inadequate preparation usually leads to ineffective practice. The lack of coverage of the disorder at undergraduate level, and in continuing professional development seems to leave teachers unprepared for the situation they may encounter in the classroom. Up-to-date clinical and scientific knowledge of ADHD is not covered adequately during the education and training of special teachers. This results in much confusion among teachers engaged in educational support, even amongst those teachers who have experience to teach children with ADHD (Akram et al., 2009). It has been found that qualified teachers also do not have adequate knowledge and understanding of the disorder and different kinds of intervention measures used (Akram et al., 2009).

Lacking knowledge about ADHD, and recognizing their own limitations, teachers are eager to learn about ADHD. They desire for more education and training in ADHD, as shown in several studies (Jerome, Gordon, & Hustler, 1994; Bekle, 2004; Holowenko & Pashute, 2000) and are also receptive to more education and information about the disorder (Akram et al., 2009). Some of them may resort to own means and search internet or media, or turn to friends for seeking information (Akram et al., 2009), due to paucity of training course and programmes related to ADHD.

To address the need of school teachers, teacher education departments have to come forward for their professional development. "Professional development is a critical support for all teachers and is necessary to student growth and achievement" (Billingsley, 2004, p. 374). This holds more true in the case of ADHD and teachers dealing with such student. Intensive and specific professional development activities should be offered to school teachers when their qualification and experiences do not match the teaching tasks which they have been assigned. The beginning special school teacher face a lot of hurdle. They have to manage many responsibilities, for example, instruction, resources, time management, bureaucratic responsibilities and work with administrators. This managing of responsibilities has to be learned through teacher education courses or programmes. Highly qualified teachers significantly increase student achievement (Darling-Hammond & Youngs, 2002).

So, teacher education departments have to organize short term diploma programs on ADHD for preparing the school teachers, in collaboration with professionals from other fields like medicine, psychiatry, and child psychology. These short term courses should provide the required knowledge, understanding and training to the teachers. Darling-Hammond (1995) stressed that effective professional development must be connected to and derived from teachers' work with their students, and be "ongoing, intensive, and supported by modelling, coaching, and the collective solving of specific problems of practice " (p. 598, as cited by Billingsley, 2004).

SUMMARY

Several intervention approaches are there for ADHD. But no single intervention or treatment is the answer for every child with ADHD. Sometimes a combination of these are required depending upon the difficulties experienced by the child and the learning content. Medicinal, psycho-social, educational and multimodel interventions are there for ADHD. Stimulants are typically used in medication for ADHD. Medications do not cure ADHD, they only control the symptoms temporarily. Psycho-social interventions employ behavioural and cognitive behavioural strategies to teach children the skills necessary to pay attention, engage in self-control, and reduce or, better modulate execessive motor activity. Psychosocial intervention include behaviour management, structured classroom management programmes, and training in social and cognitive skills. Educational intervention enable children with ADHD to gain maximally from classroom instruction and other teaching learning situations in school, and/or home. Classroom management programmes, behaviour modification techniques, cognitive-behavioural strategies and peer tutoring are used in schools and are effective with ADHD children. Researchers have ingenuously devised ways for academic intervention for children with ADHD. Multimodel treatment- a combination of different interventions, is also employed to bring desirable effect. Involvement of parents in interventions is important to produce effective results.

Bibliography

Abikoff, H. (1991). Cognitive Training in ADHD Children : Less to It Than Meets the Eye. *Journal of Learning Disabilities*, 24, 205-209.

Abikoff, H. A. & Gittleman, R. (1985). Hyperactive Children Treated with Stimulants. *Archives of General Psychiatry*, 42, 953-961.

Achenbach, T.M. & Edelbrock, C.S. (1983). *Child Behaviour Checklist Parent-Report Form*, Burlington, V.T. : University of Vermont.

Achenbach, T.M. & Edelbrock, C.S. (1986a). *Child Behaviour Checklist-Teacher Report Form*, Burlington, V.T. : University of Vermont.

Achenbach, T.M. & Edelbrock, C.S. (1986b). *Child Behaviour Checklist-Youth Self report*, Burlington, V.T. : University of Vermont.

Ackerman, P., Anhalt, J., Holcomb, P., & Dykman, R. (1986). Presumably innate and Acquired Automatic Processes in Children with Attention and/or Reading Disorders. *Journal of child Psychology and Psychiatry*, 27, 513-529.

Adams, W., Sheslow, D., Robins, P., Payne, H., & Wilkinson, G. (1991, August). *Memory Abilities in Children with Attention Deficit Hyperactivity Disorder.* Paper presented at the meeting of the American Psychological Association, San Francisco, CA.

Akram, G., Thomson, A. H., Boyter, A. C. & McLarty, M. (2009). ADHD and the Role of Medication : Knowledge and Perceptions of Qualified and Student Teachers. *European Journal of Special Needs Education*, 24, 4, 423-436.

Alessandri, S.M. (1992). Attention, Play, and Social Behaviour in ADHD Preschoolers. *Journal of Abnormal Child Psychology*, 20, 289-302.

Alloway, T. P, Rajendran, G., & Archibald, L.M.D. (2009). Working Memory in Children with Developmental Disorders. *Journal of Learning Disabilities*, 42, 4, 372-382.

Alloway, T.P. (2007). *The Automated Working Memory Assessment*. London: Pearson Assessment.

Alloway, T.P., & Archibald, L. (2008). Working Memory and Learning in Children with Developmental Coordination Disorder and Specific Language Impairment. *Journal of Learning Disabilities*, 41, 3, 251-262.

Al-Yagon, M. & Mikulincer, M. (2004). Socio-emotional and Academic Adjustment Among Children with Learning Disorders : The Mediational Role of Attachment Based Factors. *Journal of Special Education*. 38, 111-123.

Al-Yagon, M. (2003). Children at Risk for Developing Learning Disorders: Multiple Perspectives. *Journal of Learning Disabilities*, 36, 318-335.

Al-Yagon, M. (2007). Socio-emotional and Behavioural Adjustment Among School Age Children with Learning Disabilities : The Moderating Role of Maternal Personal Resources. *Journal of Special Education*, 40, 205-217.

Al-Yagon, M. (2009). Comorbid LD and ADHD in Childhood: Socio-emotional and Behavioural Adjustment and Parents Positive and Negative Affect. *European Journal of Special Needs Education*, 24, 4, 371-391.

American Psychiatric Association (1968). *Diagnostic and statistical manual of mental disorders*, (2nd ed.). Washington, DC : Author.

American Psychiatric Association (1987). *Diagnostic and Statistical manual of mental disorders* (3rd rev. ed.) Washington, DC : Author.

American Psychiatric Association (1994). *Diagnostic and statistical manual of mental disorders* (4th ed.) Washington, DC : Author.

American Psychiatric Association (1994). *Diagnostic and Statistical manual of mental disorders* (4th ed.) Washington, DC : Author.

American Psychiatric Association (2000). *Diagnostic and statistical manual of mental disorders* (4th ed., Rev.). Washington, D.C. : Author.

American Psychiatric Association. (1980). *Diagnostic and Statistical manual of mental disorders* (3rd ed.) Washington, DC : Author.

Anastopoulos, A.D. (1996). Facilitating Prental Understanding and Management of Attention Deficit and Hyperactivity Disorder. In

M.A. Reinecke, F.M. Dattilio, & A. Freeman (Eds.), *Cognitive Therapy with Children and Adolescents: A Casebook for Clinical Practice* (pp.327-343). New York : Guilford Press.

Anastopoulos, A.D., Shelton, T., Du Paul, G.J., & Gouvremont, D.C. (1993). Parent Training for Attention Deficit Hyperactivity Disorder : Its Impact on Parent Functioning. *Journal of Abnormal Child Psychology*, 21, 581 – 596.

Anderson, J. (1996). Is Childhood Hyperactivity the Product of Western ? *The Lancet*, 348, 73 -74.

Anderson, P. (2002). Assessment and Development of Executive Function (EF) During Childhood. *Child Neuropsychology*, 8, 71-82.

Angold, A., Erkanli, A., Egger, H.L., & Costello, E.J. (2000). Stimulant Treatment for Children : A Community Perspective. *Journal of the American Academy of Child and Adolescent Psychiatry*, 39, 975-984.

August, G.J. (1987). Production Deficiencies in Free Recall : A Comparison of Hyperactivity Learning Disabled and Normal Children. *Journal of Abnormal Child Psychology*, 15, 429 – 440.

August, G.J., & Garfinkel, B.D. (1990). Comorbidity of ADHD and Reading Disability Among Clinic-referred Children. *Journal of Abnormal Child Psychology*, 18, 29-45.

Aylward, E.H., Reiss, A.L., Reader, M.J., Singer, H.S., Brown, J.E., & Denckla, M.B. (1996). Basal Ganglia Volumes in Children with ADHD. *Journal of Child Neurology*, 11, 112-115.

Aylward, G.P., Gordon, M., & Verhulst, S.J. (1997). Relationships Between Continuous Performance Task Scores and Other Cognitive Measures: Causality or Commonality? *Assessment*, 4, 4, 325-336.

Baddeley, A. D. (1986). *Working Memory*. Oxford, UK : Clarendon.

Baddeley, A.D., & Hitch, G. (1974). Working Memory. In G.A. Bower (Ed.) *The Psychology of Learning and Motivation : Advances in Research and Theory* (Vol. 8, pp. 47-89). New York : Academic Press.

Baddeley, A.D., & Logie, R.H. (1999). Working Memory: The Multiple - component Model. In A. Miyake & P. Shah (Eds.), *Models of Working Memory : Mechanisms of Active Maintenance and Executive Control* (pp. 26-61). New York : Cambridge University Press.

Barbaresi, W.J., & Olsen, R.D. (1998). An ADHD Educational Intervention for Elementary School Teachers : A pilot study. *Developmental and Behavioural Paediatrics*, 19, 94-100.

Barkley, R. (1997a). *ADHD and the Nature of Self-control*. New York : Guilford Press.

Barkley, R. A. (1998a). *Attention-deficit Hyperactivity-disorder. A Handbook for diagnosis and treatment* (2nd ed.), New York : Guilford Press.

Barkley, R. A. (2000b). *Taking Charge of ADHD.* New York : The Guilford Press, p. 21.

Barkley, R., Anastopoulas, A., Guevremont, D., Fletcher, K. (1991). Adolescents with ADHD : Patterns of Behavioural Adjustment, Academic Functioning, and Treatment Utilization. *Journal of the Americal Academy of Child and Adolescent Psychiatry,* 30, 752-761.

Barkley, R.A. & Edwards, G. (1998). Diagnostic Interview, Behaviour Rating Scales and the Medical Examination. In R.A. Barkley (Ed.) *Attention Deficit Hyperactivity Disorder* (pp. 263 – 293), New York : Guilford.

Barkley, R.A. & Murphy, K.R. (1998). *Attention Deficit Hyperactivity Disorder: A Clinical Workbook* (2nd ed.), New York : Guilford.

Barkley, R.A. (1990). *Attention Deficit Hyperactivity Disorder : A Handbook for Diagnosis and Treatment,* New York : Guilford.

Barkley, R.A. (1995). *Taking Charge of ADHD : The Complete Authoritative Guide for Parents.* New York : Guilford Press.

Barkley, R.A. (1996). Attention Deficit/Hyperactivity Disorder. In E.J. Mash & R.A. Barkley (Eds.), *Child Psycho-pathology* (pp. 63 – 112). New York: Guilford Press.

Barkley, R.A. (1997b). Behavioural Inhibition, Sustained Attention and Executive Functions : Constructing a Unifying Theory of ADHD. *Psychological Bulletin,* 121, 65-94.

Barkley, R.A. (1997c). Attention-deficit Hyperactivity Disorder. In E. Mash & L. Terdal (Eds.), *Assessment of Childhood Disorders* (3rd ed., pp. 71–129). New York : Guilford.

Barkley, R.A. (1998b). *Attention Deficit Hyperactivity Disorder,* New York : Guilford.

Barkley, R.A. (2000a). Genetics of Childhood Disorders : XVII. ADHD, Part 1; The Executive Functions and ADHD. *Journal of the American Academy of Child and Adolescent Psychiatry,* 39, 1064-1068.

Barkley, R.A. (2006). *Attention -deficit hyperactivity disorder : A handbook for diagnosis and treatment* (3rd ed) . New York : Guilford.

Barkley, R.A., Fischer, M., Edelbrock, C. & Smallish, L. (1991). The Adolescent Outcome of Hyperactive Children Diagnosed by Research Criteria – III : Mother-child Interactions, Family Conflicts and Maternal Psycho-pathology. *Journal of Child Psychology and Psychiatry,* 32, 233 – 255.

Barkley, R.A., Fischer, M., Edelbrock, C.S., & Smallish, L. (1990). The Small Adolescent Outcome of Hyperactive Children Diagnosed by Research Criteria : An 8-year Prospective Study. *Journal of American Academy of Child & Adolescent Psychiatry*, 29, 88-95.

Barkley, R.A., Fischer, M., Smallish, L., & Fletcher, K. (2002). The Persistence of Attention Deficit/Hyperactivity Disorder into Young Adulthood as a Function of Reporting Source and Definition of Disorder. *Journal of Abnormal Child Psychology* 111, 279- 289.

Barkley, R.A., Grodzinsky, G., & DuPaul, G. J. (1992). Frontal Lobe Functions in Attention Deficit Disorder with and Without Hyperactivity : A Review and Research Report. *Journal of Abnormal Child Psychology*, 20, 163-188.

Barkley, R.A., McMurray, M.B., Edelbrock, C., & Robbins, K. (1990). Side Effects of Methylphenidate in Children with Attention Deficit Hyperactivity Disorder : A Systemic Placebo-controlled Evaluation. *Paediatrics*, 86, 184–192.

Barnett, R., Maruff, P., Vance, A., Luk, W.S., Costin, J., Wood, C. et al. (2001). Abnormal Executive Function in Attention Deficit Hyperactivity Disorder. The Effect of Stimulant Medication and Age on Spatial Working Memory. *Psychological Medicine*, 31, 1107-1115.

Barrouillet, P., Fayol, M., & Lathuliere, E. (1997). Selecting Between Competititors in Multiplication Tasks : An Explanation of the Errors Produced by Adolescents with Learning Disabilities. *International Journal of Behavioural Development*, 21, 253-275.

Barry, T.D., Lyman, R.D., & Klinger, L.G. (2002). Academic Underachievement and Attention Deficit/Hyperactivity Disorder. The Negative Impact of Symptom Severity on School Performance. *Journal of School Psychology*, 40, 259 – 283

Bauermeister, J.J. (1992). Factor Analysis of Teacher Ratings of Attention Deficit hyperactivity and Oppositional Defiant Symptoms in Children Aged Four Through Thirteen Years. *Journal of Clinical Child Psychology*, 21, 27-34.

Bauermeister, J.J., Bird, H.R., Canino, G., Rubio-stipec, M., Bravo, M. & Algeria, M. (1995). Dimensions of Attention Deficit Hyperactivity Disorder : Findings from Teacher and Parent Reports in a Community Sample. *Journal of Consulting and Clinical Psychology*, 24, 264-271.

Baum, S.M., Olenchak, F. R., & Owen, S. F. (1998). Gifted students with Attention Deficits : Fact and/or Fiction? *Gifted Child Quarterly*, 42, 96-104.

Baumgaertel, A., Wolraich, M.L., & Dietrich, M. (1995) . Comparison of Diagnostic Criteria for Attention Deficit Disorders in a German Elementary School Sample. *Journal of the American Academy of Child and Adolescent Psychiatry*, 34, 629-638.

Bekle, B. (2004). Knowledge and Attitudes about ADHD: A Comparison Between Practising Teachers and Undergraduate Education Students. *Journal of Attention Disorders*, 7, 151-161.

Benedetto-Nasho, B. & Tannock, R. (1999). Math Computation, Error Patterns and Stimulant Effect in Children with Attention Deficit Hyperactivity Disorder. *Journal of Attention Disorders*, 3, 121-134.

Bhatia, M.S., Nigam, V.R., Bohra, N. & Malik, S.C. (1991). Attention Deficit Disorder with Hyperactivity Among Pediatric Outpatient. *Journal of Child Psychology and Psychiatry*, 32, 297-306.

Bickett, L., & Milich, R. (1990). First Impressions Formed of Boys with Learning Disabilities and Attention Deficit Disorder. *Journal of Learning Disabilities*, 23, 253 – 259.

Biederman, J., Faraone, S. V., & Kiely, K. (1996). Comorbidity in Outcome of Attention-deficit/Hyperactivity Disorder. In L. Hechtman (Ed.), *Do They Grow Out of It? Long-term Outcomes of Childhood Disorders* (pp. 39-75). Washington, DC:American Psychiatric Press.

Biederman, J., Faraone, S.V., Keenan, K., Knee, D., & Tsuang, M.F. (1990). Family Genetic and Psychosocial Risk Factors in DSM-III Attention Deficit Disorder. *Journal of the American Academy of Child and Adolescent Psychiatry*, 29, 4, 526 – 533.

Biederman, J., Mick, E., & Faraone, S.V. (2000). Age-dependent Decline of Symptoms of Attention Deficit Hyperactivity Disorder : Impact of Remission Definition and Symptom Type. *American Journal of Psychiatry*, 157, 816-818.

Biederman, J., Milberger, S., Faraone, S.V., Keily, K., Guite, J., Mick, E., Ablon, S., Warburton, R., & Reed, E. (1995). Family-environment Risk Factors for Attention-deficit Hyperactivity Disorder. *Archives of General Psychiatry*, 52, 464-470.

Biederman, J., Monuteaux, M.C., & Doyle, A.E. (2004). Impact of Executive Function Deficits and Attention-deficit Hyperactivity Disorder (ADHD) on Academic Outcomes in Children. *Journal of Consulting and Clinical Psychology*, 72 (5), 757-766.

Biederman, J., Rosenbaum, J.F., Bolduc-Murphy, E.A., Faraone, S.V., Chaloff, J., Hirshfeld, D.R., & Kagan, J. (1993). A 3-year Follow-up of Children With and Without Behavioural Inhibition. *Journal of American Academy of Child and Adolescent Psychiatry*, 32, 814 – 821.

Biederman, J., Wilens, T., Mick, E., & Faraone, S.V. (1997). Is ADHD A Risk Factor for Psychoactive Substance Use Disorders ? Findings from a Four-year Prospective Follow-up Study. *Journal of the American Academy of Child & Adolescent Psychiatry*, 36, 21-29.

Biederman, J., Wilens, T., Mick, E., Spencer, T., & Faraone, S. V. (1999). Pharmacotherapy of Attention Deficit/Hyperactivity Disorder Reduces Risk for Substance Use Disorder. *Paediatrics*, 104, e 20.

Billingsley, B.S. (2004). Promoting Teacher Quality and Retention in Special Education. *Journal of Learning Disabilities*, 37, 5, 370-376.

Bird, H. R. (2002). The Diagnostic Classification, Epidemiology and Cross-Cultural Validity of ADHD. In P.S. Jensen & J. R. Cooper (Eds.), *Attention Deficit Hyperactivity Disorder : State of Science/Best Practices*. Kingston, NJ : Civic Research Institute.

Bonafina, M. A., Newcorn, J. H., Mckay, K. E., Koda, V. H., & Halperin, J. M. (2000). ADHD and Reading Disabilities. A Cluster Analytic Approach for Distinguishing Subgroups. *Journal of Learning Disabilities*, 33, 297-307.

Boonstra, A.M., Oosterlaan, J., Sergeant, J.A., & Buitelaar, J. K. (2005). Executive Functioning in Adult ADHD : A Meta-analytic Review. *Psychological Medicine*, 35, 1097-1108.

Bradley, K.L. & DuPaul, G.J. (1997). Attention Deficit/Hyperactivity Disorder. In G.G. Bear, K.M. Minke, and A. Thomas (Eds.), *Children's needs II : Development, problems and alternatives* (pp. 109-117). Bethesda, MD : National Association of School Psychologists.

Braswell, L. & Bloomquist, M.L. (1991). *Cognitive Behavioural Therapy with ADHD Children: Child, Family and School Interventions*, New York: Guilford Press.

Braswell, L. (1991). Involving Parents in Cognitive Behavioural Therapy with Children and Adolescents. In P.C. Kendall (Ed.), *Child and Adolescent Therapy : Cognitive Behavioural Procedures* (pp. 316-351). New York: Guilford Press.

Bridgett, D.J., & Walker, M.E. (2006). Intellectual Functioning in Adults with ADHD : A Meta-analytic Examination of Full Scale IQ Differences Between Adults with and Without ADHD. *Psychological Assessment*, 18, 1-14.

Burnett, R., & Kastman, L. (1997). Teaching Composition : Current Theories and Practice. In G. Phye (Ed.), *Handbook of Academic Learning: Construction of Knowledge* (pp. 268-305). Sandiego : Academic Press.

Burns, G.L., Walsh, J.A. & Gomez, R. (2003). Convergent and Discriminate Validity of Trait and Source Effects in ADHD-inattention and

Hyperactivity/Impulsivity Measures Across a 3-month Interval. *Journal of Abnormal Child Psychology,* 31, 529-541.

Burns, G.L., Walsh, J.A., Owen, S.M., & Snell, J., (1997). The Internal Validity of the DSM-III-R and DSM-IV Disruptive Behaviour Disorder Symptoms : Implications from Teacher Ratings for a Dimensional Approach to a Symptoms Validity. *Journal of Child Clinical Psychology,* 26, 266-275.

Bussing, R., Schoenberg, N.E., & Perwien, A.R. (1998). Knowledge and information about ADHD : Evidence of cultural differences among African-American and Caucasian parents. *Social Science and Medicine,* 46, 919-928.

Bussing, R., Schoenberg, N.E., Rogers, K.M., Zima, B.T., & Angus, S. (1998). Explanatory models of ADHD : Do they differ by ethnicity, child gender, or treatment status? *Journal of Emotional and Behavioural Disorders,* 6, 233-242.

Cantwell, D.P. (1987, June). *Assessment and invention.* Paper presented at the conference 'The nature of the ADHD'. Minneapolis, MN.

Carlson, C.L., Lahey, B.B., & Neeper, R. (1986). Direct assessment of the cognitive correlates of attention deficit disorders with and without hyperactivity. *Journal of Psychopathological Behaviour Assessment,* 8, 69-86.

Casey, B.J., Castellanos, F.X., Giedd, J.N., Marsh, W.L., Hamburger, S.D., Schubert, A.B., et al. (1997). Implication of Right Frontostriatal Circuitry in Response Inhibition and Attention Deficit/Hyperactivity Disorder. *Journal of the American Academy of Child and Adolescent Psychiatry,* 36, 374-383.

Castellanos, F.X., Giedd, J.N., Eckburg, P., Marsh, W.L., Vaituzis, A.C., Kaysen, D., et al. (1994). Quantitative Morphology of the Caudate Nucleus in Attention Deficit Hyperactivity Disorder. *American Journal of Psychiatry,* 151, 1791-1796.

Castellanos, F.X., Lee, P.P., Sharp, W., Jeffries, N.O., Greenstein, D.K., Clasen, L.S., Blumenthal, J.D., James, R.S., Ebens, C.I., Walter, J.M., Zijdenbos, A., Evans, A.C., Giedd, J.N., & Rapoport, J.L. (2002). Developmental Trajectories of Brain Volume Abnormalities in Children and Adolescents with Attention Deficit/Hyperactivity Disorder. *Journal of the American Medical Association,* 288, 14, 1740-1748.

Children with Attention Deficit Disorders. (1992). The Teacher's Challenge, *The CH.A.D.D.ER Box,* 5(7), 14-15.

Clark, C., Prior, M., & Kinsella, G. (2002). The Relationship Between Executive Function Abilities, Adaptive Behaviour, and academic

Achievement in Children with Externalizing Behaviour Problems. *Journal of Child Psychology and Psychiatry*, 43, 785-796.

Clarke, L., Ungerer, J., Chahoud, K., Johnson, S., and Stiefel, I. (2002). Attention Deficit hyperactivity Disorder is Associated with attachment Insecurity. *Clinical Child Psychology and Psychiatry*, 7, 179-198.

Comings, D.E., Comings, B.G., Muhleman, L., Dietz, G., Shahbahrami, B., Tast, D., et al., (1991). The Dopamine D2 Receptor Gene as a Modifying Gene in Neuropsychiatric Diorders. *Journal of the American Clinical Association*, 266, 1793-1800.

Compas, B.E. (1997). Depression in Children And adolescents. In E.J. Mash & L.G. Terdal (Eds.), *Assessment of Childhood Disorders* (3rd Ed.; pp. 197-229). New York : Guilford.

Conners, C.K. (1980). *Food Additives and Hyperactive Children.* New York : Plenum Press.

Conners, C.K. (1990). *The Conners Rating Scales.* North Tonawanda, NY: Multi-Health Systems.

Conners, C.K. (1992). *Continuous Performance test Computer Programme : User's Guide.* North Tonawanda, NY: MHS.

Conners, C.K., Erhardt, D., Epstein, J.N., Parker, J.D., Sitarenios, G., & Sparrow, E. (1999) . Self-ratings of ADHD Symptoms in Adults : I. Factor Structure and Normative Data. *Journal of Attention Disorders*, 3, 141-151.

Conners, C.K., Parker, J.D.A., Sitarenios, G., & Epstein, J.N. (1998). The Revised Conners' Parent Rating Scales (CPRS-R) : Factor Structure, Reliability, and Criterion Validity. *Journal of Abnormal Child Psychology*, 26, 257-268.

Conners, C.K., Sitarenios, G., Parker, J.D., & Epstein, J.N. (1998 a). Revision and Restandardization of the Conners Parent Rating Scales (CPRS-R): Factor Structure, Reliability, and Criterion Validity. *Journal of Abnormal Child Psychology*, 26, 257-268.

Conners, C.K., Sitarenios, G., Parker, J.D., & Epstein, J.N. (1998b). Revision and Restandardization of the Conners Teacher Rating Scale (CTRS-R) : Factor structure, Reliability, and Criterion Validity. *Journal of Abnormal Child Psychology*, 26, 279-291.

Cook, E.H., Stein, M.A., Krasowski, M.D., Cox, N.J., Olkon, D.M., Kieffer, J., & Leventhal, B. (1995). Association of Attention Deficit Disorder and the Dopamine Transporter Gene. *Americal Journal of Human Genetics*, 56, 993-998.

Cooley, E. L., & Morris, R. D. (1990). Attention in children : A Neuropsychologically Based Model for assessment. *Developmental Neuropsychology*, 6, 3, 239-274.

Cooper, P., & Bilton, K. (2002). *ADHD A Practical Guide for Teachers*. 2nd ed. London : David Fulton Publishers.

Cooper, P., & O' Regan, F. (2001). *Educating Children with ADHD : A Teacher's Manual*. London : Routledge/Falmer.

Cowan, N. (1995). *Attention and Memory : An Integrated Framework*. Oxford, U.K. : Oxford University Press.

Crinella, F. M., & Yu, J. (2000). Brain Mechanisms and Intelligence : Psychometric g and Executive Function. *Intelligence*, 27, 299-237.

Darling-Hammond, L. & Youngs, P. (2002). Defining "highly qualified Teachers" : What Does "Scientifically. Based Research" Actually Tell Us? *Educational Researcher*, 31, 9, 1-13.

Darling-Hammond, L. (1995). Policies that Support Professional Development in an Era of Reform *Phi Delta Kappan*, 76, 597-604.

Dawson, P. & Guare, R. (2004). *Executive Skills in Children and Adolescents*: A Practical Guide to Assessment and Intervention. New York: Guilford.

De La Paz, S. (2001). Teaching Writing to Students with Attention Deficit Disorders and Specific Language Impairment. *The Journal of Educational Research*, 95, 37-47.

Denckla, M., & Rudel, R. (1978). Anomalies of Motor Development in Hyperactive Boys. *Annals of Neurology*, 3, 231-233.

Denckla, M.B. (1995). A Theory and Model of Executive Function : A neur opsychological Perspective. In G. R. Lyon & N. A. Krasnegor (Eds.) , *Attention, Memory, and Executive Function* (pp. 263-277). Baltimore : Brookes.

Denckla, M.B., & Reiss, A.L. (1997). Pre frontal Subcortical Circuits in Developmental Disorders. In N.A. Krasnegor, G.R. Lyon & P.S. Goldman Rakic (Eds.), *Development of the Pre frontal Cortex : Evolution, Ueurobiology, and Behaviour* (pp. 265-282). Baltimore : Brookes.

DeShazo, B.T., Lyman, R.D., & Klinger, L.G. (2002). Academic Underachievement and Attention Deficit/Hyperactivity Disorder. The Negative Impact of Symptom Severity on School Performance. *Journal of School Psychology*, 40, 3, 259-283.

Deutsch, K. (1987). Genetic Factors in Attention Deficit Disorder: Paper presented at Symposium on Disorders of Brain and Development and Cognition, Boston, M.A. As cited in Barkley, R., & Anastopoulas, A. (1988). Biological Factors in Attention Deficit Hyperactivity Disorder. *The Behaviour Therapist.* 11, 47-53.

Dewey, D., Kaplan, B., Crawford, S. & Fisher, G. (1998). Predictive Accuracy of the Wide Range Assessment of Memory and Learning in Children with Attention Deficit Hyperactivity Disorder and Reading Difficulties. *Developmental Neuropsychology*, 19, 173-189.

Disney, E. R., Elkins, I. J., McGue, M., & Iacono, W.G. (1999). Effects of ADHD, Conduct Disorder, and Gender on Substance Use and Abuse in Adolescence. *American Journal of Psychiatry*, 156, 1515-1521.

Douglas, V. I. (1988). Cognitive Deficits in Children with Attention Deficit Disorder with Hyperactivity. In L. M. Bloomingdale & J. A. Sergeant (Eds.), *Attention Deficit Disorder : Criteria, Cognition, Intervention* (pp. 65-82). London : Pergamon Press.

Douglas, V.I. (1983). Attention and Cognitive Problems. In M. Rutter (Ed.), *Developmental Neuropsychiatry* (pp. 280-329) New York : Guilford Press.

Douglas, V.I., Barr, R. G., Amin, K., O'Neill, M.E., & Britton, B. G. (1988). Dosage Effects and Individual Responsivity to Methylphenidate in Attention Deficit Disorder. *Journal of Child Psychology and Psychiatry*, 29, 453-475.

Downey, K.K., Stelson, F.W., Pomerleau, O.F. & Giordani, B. (1997). Adult Attention Deficit Hyperactivity Disorder. Psychological test Profiles in a Clinical Population. *Journal of Nervous and Mental Disease*, 185, 32-38.

Doyle, A.E., Biederman, J., Seidman, L. F., Weber, W., & Faraone, S. V. (2000) Diagnostic Efficiency of Neuro-psychological Test Scores for Discriminating Boys With and Without Attention Deficit-hyperactivity Disorder. *Journal of Consulting and Clinical Psychology*, 68, 477-488.

DSM-IV-TR Work Group. *The Diagnostic and Statistical Manual of Mental Disorders* (Fourth edition), Text Revision, Washington, DC : American Psychiatric Association.

Du Paul, G.J. & Henningson, P.N. (1993). Peer Tutoring Effects on the Classroom Performance of Children with Attention Deficit Hyperactivity Disorder. *School Psychology Review*, 22, 134-143.

Du Paul, G.J., & Stoner, G. (1994). *ADHD in the Schools. Assessment and Intervention Strategies.* New York : Guilford Press.

Du Paul, G.J., Power, T.J., Anastopoulos, A.D., & Reid, R. (1998). *ADHD Rating Scale-IV : Checklists, Norms and Clinical Interpretation,* New York: Guilford.

DuPaul, G.J. & Eckert, T.L. (1997). The Effects of School based Interventions for Attention Deficit Hyperactivity Disorder : A Meta Analysis. *School Psychology Review*, 26, 1, 5-27.

DuPaul, G.J. & Eckert, T.L. (1998). Academic Interventions for Students with Attention Deficit/ Hyperactivity Disorder:A Review of the Literature: *Reading and Writing Quarterly : Overcoming Learning Difficulties*, 14, 59-82.

DuPaul, G.J., Anastopoulos, A.D., McGoey, K.E., Power, T.J., Reid, R., & Ikeda, M.J. (1997). Teacher Ratings of Attention Deficit Hyperactivity Disorder Symptoms : Factor Atructure and Normative Data. *Psychological Assessment*, 9, 436-444.

DuPaul, G.J., Anastopoulos, A.D., Power, T.J., Reid, R., Ikeda, M.J., & McGoey, K.E. (1998a). Parent Ratings of Attention Deficit/ Hyperactivity Disorder Symptoms : Factor Structure and Normative Data. *Journal of Psycho-pathology and Behavioural Assessment*, 20, 83-102.

DuPaul, G.J., Schaughency, E.A., Weyandt, L.L., Tripp, G., Kiesner, J., Ota, K., & Stanish, H. (2001). Self-report of ADHD symptoms in university students : Cross gender and cross national prevalence. *Journal of Learning Disabilities*, 34, 4, 370-379.

Edelbrock, C., Costello, A. J., & Kessler, M. D. (1984). Empirical Corroboration of the Attention Deficit Disorder. *Journal of the American Academy of Child and Adolescent Psychiatry*, 23, 285-290.

Elia, J., Ambrosini, P., & Berrettini, W. (2008). ADHD Characteristics: I. Concurrent Co-morbidity patterns in Children and adolescents. *Child and Adolescent Psychiatry and Mental Health*, 2, 1, 15.

Elkins, J. (2000). Numeracy. In A.F. Ashman & J. Elkins (Eds.), *Educating Children with Diverse Abilities* (pp. 436-469). Frenchs Forest, NSW, Australia : Pearson Education.

Ercan E.S., Coskunol, H., Varan, A., & Toksoz, K. (2003). Childhood Attention Deficit/Hyperactivity Disorder and Alcohol Dependence : A 1 year Follow-up. *Alcohol & Alcoholism*, 38, 352-356.

Faraone, S., Biederman, J., Krifcher Lehman, B., Keenan, K., Norman, D., Seidman, L., et al. (1993). Evidence for the Independent Familial Transmission of Attention Deficit Hyperactivity Disorder and Learning diabilities : Results from a Family Genetic Study. *American Journal of Psychiatry*, 150, 891-895.

Farrington, D. P. (1991). Childhood Aggression and Adult Violence : Early Precursors and Life Outcomes. In D. J. Pepler & K. H. Rubin (Eds.),

The Development and Treatment of Childhood Aggression. (pp. 5-29). Hillsdale, NJ : Erlbaum.

Feingold, B.F. (1975). *Why Your Child is Hyperactive.* New York : Random House.

Felton, R.H., & Wood, F.B. (1989) . Cognitive Deficits in Reading Disability and Attention Deficit Disorder. *Journal of Learning Disabilities,* 22, 3-13.

Filipek, P. A., Semrud - Clikeman, M., Steingard, R. J., Renshaw, P. F., Kennedy, D. N., & Biederman, J. (1997). Volumetric MRI Analysis Comparing Participants Having Attention Deficit Hyperactivity Disorder with Normal Controls. *Neurology,* 48, 589-601.

Fischer, J.M., Barkley, R.A., Fletcher, K.A., & Smallish, L. (1993). The Adolescent Outcome of Hyperactive Children : Predictors of Psychiatric, Academic, Social, and Emotional Adjustment. *Journal of the American Academy of Child and Adolescent Psychiatry,* 32, 324-332.

Fischer, M. (1997). The persistence of ADHD into Adulthood : It Depends on Whom You Ask. *ADHD Report,* 5, 8-10

Fischer, M., Barkley, R.A., Edelbrock, C.S., & Smallish, L. (1990). The Adolescent Outcome of Hyperactive Children Diagnosed by Research Criteria : Academic, Attentional and neuro-psychological Status. *Journal of Consulting and Clinical Psychology,* 58, 580-588.

Fitzgerald, G., Fick, L., & Milich, R. (1986). Computer Assisted Instruction for Students with Attentional Difficulties. *Journal of Learning Disabilities,* 19, 376-379.

Fletcher, J. M. (Ed.). (1996). Executive Functions in Children [Special issue]. *Developmental Neuropsychology,* 12, 1-128.

Folstein, S.E., Brandt, J., & Folstein, M. (1990). Huntington's Disease. In J.L. Cummings (Ed.), *Subcortical Dementia* (pp. 87-107). New York: Oxford University Press.

Forness, S.R., Youpa, D., Hanna, G.L., Cantwell, D.P., & Swanson, J.M. (1992). Classroom Instructional Characteristics in Attention Deficit Hyperactivity Disorder : Comparison of Pure and Mixed Groups. *Behavioural Disorders,* 17, 115-125.

Frazier, T.W., Demaree, H.A., & Youngstrom, E.A. (2004). Meta-analysis of Intellectual and Neuro-psychological Test Performance in Attention-deficit/Hyperactivity Disorder. *Neuro-psychology,* 18, 543-555.

Frazier, T.W., Youngstrom, E.A., Glutting, J.J. & Watkins, M.W. (2007). ADHD and Achievement : Meta-analysis of the Child, Adolescent, and Adult Literatures and a Concomitant Study with College Students. *Journal of Learning Disabilities*, 40, 1, 49-65.

Frith, U. (1985). Beneath the Surface of Surface Dyslexia. In J. C. Marshall, M. Coltheart, & K. Patterson (Eds.), *Surface Dyslexia and Surface Dysgraphia* (pp. 310-330). London : Routledge & Kegan Paul.

Gathercole, S. E. & Baddeley, A.D. (1993) . *Working Memory and Language.* Hillsdale, NJ : Erlbaum.

Gathercole, S.E., & Alloway, T. P. (2008). *Working Memory and Learning:* A practical guide Thousand Oaks. CA: Sage.

Gathercole, S.E., Alloway, T.P., Willis, C., & Adams, A.M. (2006). Working Memory in Children with Literacy and Mathematical Difficulties. *Journal of Experimental Child Psychology*, 93, 265-281.

Gaub, M., & Carlson, C.L. (1997 a). Gender Differences in ADHD : A Meta-analysis and Critical Review. *Journal of the American Academy of Child & Adolescent Psychiatry*, 36, 1036-1045.

Gaub, M. & Carlson, C. L. (1997b). Behavioual Characteristics of DSM-IV ADHD Subtypes in a school-based Population. *Journal of Abnormal Child Psychology*, 25, 103 – 111.

Geary, D.C. (2004). Mathematics and Learning Disabilities. *Journal of Learning Disabilties*, 37, 4-15.

Geary, D.C., Hamson, C.O., & Hoard, M.K. (2000). Numerical and Arithmetic Cognition : A Longitudinal Study of Process and Concept Deficits in Children with Learning Disability. *Journal of Experimental Child Psychology*, 77, 236-263.

Gershon, J. (2002) A Meta-analytic Review of Gender Differences in ADHD. *Journal of Attention Disorders*, 5, 143-154.

Gilger, J.W., Pennington. B.F., & DeFries, J.C. (1992). A Twin Study of the Etiology of Comorbidity: Attention Deficit Hyperactivity Disorder and Dyslexia. *Journal of the American Academy of Child and Adolescent Psychiatry*, 31, 343-348.

Gill, M., Daly, G., Heron, S., Hawi, Z., & Fitzgerald, M. (1997). Confirmation of Association Between Attention Deficits Disorder and a Dopamine Transporter Polymorphism. *Molecular Psychiatry*, 2, 311-313.

Gittelman, R., Mannuzza, S., Shenker, R., & Bonagura, N. (1985). Hyperactive Boys Almost Grown up. *Archives of General Psychiatry*, 42, 937-947.

Glutting, J., Sheslow, D., & Adams, W. (2002). *CARE : College ADHD Response Evaluation.* Washington, DE: Wide Range.

Glutting, J.J., Monghan, M.C., Adams, W. & Sheslow, D. (2002). Some Psychometric Properties of a System to Measure ADHD Among College Students : Factor Pattern, Reliability and One-year Predictive validity. *Measurement and Evaluation in Couselling and Development*, 34, 194-208.

Goodman, S. H. & Gotlib, I.H. (2002). *Children of Depressed Parents.* Washington, DC : American Psychology Association.

Goodyear, P. & Hynd, G. (1992). Attention Deficit Disorder with (ADHD/H) and without (ADD/WO) Hyperativity : Behavioural and Neuro-psychological differentiation. *Journal of Clinical Child Psychology*, 21, 273-305.

Gordon, M., & Barkley, R.A. (1998). Tests and Observational Measures. In R.A. Barkley (Ed.), *Attention Deficit Hyperactivity Disorder* (pp. 345 – 372), New York : Guilford.

Graham, S., & Harris, K. (1989). Improving Learning Disabled Students' Skills at Composing Essays : Self Instructional Strategy Training. *Exceptional Children*, 56, 201-214.

Graham, S., & Harris, K. (2003). Students with Learning Disabilities and the Process of Writing : A Meta-analysis of SRSD Studies. In H. L. Swanson, K. R. Harris, & S. Graham (Eds.), *Handbook of Learning disabilities* (pp. 323-344). New York : Guilford.

Graham, S., & Perin, D. (2007). A meta-analysis of Writing Instruction for Adolescent Students. *Journal of Educational Psychology*, 99,3, 445-476.

Greene, R. W., Biederman, J., Faraone, S. V., & Wilens, T. (1999). Further Validation of Social Impairment as a Predictor of Substance Use Disorders : Findings from a Sample of Siblings of Boys with ADHD. *Journal of Clinical Child Psychology*, 20, [illegible].

Greene, R. W., Biederman, J., Faraone, S.V., Sienna, M., & Garcia-Jetton, J. (1997). Adolescent Outcome of Boys with Attention Deficit/Hyperactivity Disorder and Social Disability : Results from a 4-year longitudinal Follow-up study. *Journal of Consulting & Clinical Psychology*, 65, 758-767.

Greenhill, L. L. (1998). Diagonsing ADHD in Children. *Journal of Clinical Psychiatry*, 59, 31-41.

Grodzinsky, G., & Diamond, R. (1992). Frontal Lobe Functioning in Boys with Attention Deficit Hyperactivity Disorder. *Developmental Neuro-psychology*, 8, 427-445.

Gross-Tsur, V., Manor, O., & Shalev, R. S. (1996). Developmental dyscalculia: Prevalence and Demographic Features. *Developmental Medicine and Child Neurology*, 38, 25-33.

Hallowell, E. & Ratey, J. (1994). *Driven to Distraction*. New York : Simon & Schuster.

Harris, K. R., & Graham, S. (1996). *Making the Writing Process Work : Strategies for Composition and Self Regulation*. Cambridge, MA : Brookline.

Hart, E.L., Lahey, B. B., Loeber, R., Applegate, B., Green, S.M., & Frick, P. J. (1995). Developmental Change in Attention Deficit Hyperactivitiy Disorder in Boys : A Four-year Longitudinal Study. *Journal of Abnormal Child Psychology*, 23, 729 – 749.

Harvey, W.J. & Reid, G. (2003). Attention-deficit/Hyperactivity Disorder : A Review of Research on Movement Skill Performance and Physical Fitness. *Adapted Physical Activity Quarterly*, 20, 1-25.

Hayes, J. R. & Flower, L. S. (1980). Identifying the Organization of the Writing Process. In L. W. Gregg & E. R. Steinberg (Eds.), *Cognitive Processes in Writing* (pp. 3-30), Hillsdale, NJ : Lawrence Erlbaum.

Healy, J.M., Newcorn, J.H., Halperin, J.M., Wolf, L.E., Pascualvaca, D.M., Schmeidler, J., & O'Brien, J.D. (1993) . The Factor Structure of ADHD Items in DSM-III-R : Internal Consistency and External Validation. *Journal of Abnormal Child Psychology*, 21, 441-453.

Heaton, R.K. (1981). *The Wisconsin Card Sorting Test Manual*. Odessa, FL Psychological Assessment Resources.

Heiligenstein, E., Conyers, L.M., Berns, A.R., & Smith, M.A. (1998). Preliminary Normative Data on DSM-IV Attention Deficit Disorder in College Students. *Journal of American College Health*, 46, 185-188.

Heiligenstein, E., Guenther, G., Levy, A., Savino, F. & Fulwiler, J. (1999). Psychological and Academic Functioning in College Students with Attention Deficit Hyperactivity Disorder. *Journal of American College Health*, 47, 4, 181-185.

Hervey, A.S., Epstein, J. N., & Curry, J.F. (2004). Neuro-psychology of Adults with Attention Deficit/Hyperactivity Disorder : A Meta-analytic Review. *Neuro-psychology*, 18, 485-503.

Heyer, J. (1995). The Responsibilities of Speech-language Pathologists Toward Children with ADHD. *Seminars in Speech and Language*, 16, 275-288.

Hill, J.C., & Schroener, E.P. (1996). Age-dependent Decline of Symptoms of Attention Deficit Hyperactivity Disorder. *American Journal of Psychiatry*, 153, 1143-1146.

Hinshaw, S. P., Henker B., & Whalen, C.K. (1984b). Self-control in Hyperactive Boys in Anger-inducing Situations : Effects of Cognitive-behavioural Training and Methylphenidate. *Journal of Abnormal Child Psychology*, 12, 55-77.

Hinshaw, S. P., Henker, B., & Whalen, C.K. (1984a). Cognitive-behavioural and Pharmacologic Interventions for Hyperactive Boys : Comparative and Combined Effects. *Journal of Consulting and Clinical Psychology*, 52, 739-749.

Hinshaw, S.P. (1992a). Academic Underachievement, Attention Deficits, and Aggression : Comorbidity and Implications for Intervention. *Journal of Consulting and Clinical Psychology*, 60, 6, 893-903.

Hinshaw, S.P. (1992b). Externalizing Behaviour Problems and Academic Underachievement in Childhood and Adolescence : Causal Relationships and Underlying Mechanisms-*Psychological Bulletin*, 111, 127-155.

Hinshaw, S.P., & Erhardt, D. (1991). Attention-deficit Hyperactivity Disorder. In P.C. Kendall (Ed.), *Child and Adolescent therapy : Cognitive behavioral procedure*, (pp. 98-128). New York : Guilford Press.

Hinshaw, S.P., Carte, E.T., Fan, C., Jassy, J.S., & Owens, E.B. (2007). Neuro-psychological Functioning of Girls with Attention-deficit/ Hyperactivity Disorder Followed Prospectively into Adolescence : Evidence for Continuing Deficits? *Neuro-psychology*, 21, 263-273.

Hitch, G.J. (1978). The Role of Short Term Working Memory in Mental Arithmetic. *Cognitive Psychology*, 10, 302-323.

Ho, T., Leung, P.W., Luk, S.L., & Taylor, E. (1996). Establishing the Constructs of Childhood Behavioural Disturbances in a Chinese population : A Questionnaire Study. *Journal of Abnormal Child Psychology*, 24, 417-431.

Holowenko, H., & Pashute, K. (2000). ADHD in Schools : A Survey of Prevalence and Coherence Across a Local U.K. Population. *Educational Psychology in Practice*, 16, 181-191

Homatidis, S. & Konstantareas, M.M. (1981). Assessment of Hyperactivity: Isolating Measures of High Discriminant Validity. *Journal of Consulting and Clinical Psychology*. 49, 533-541.

Hoza, B., & Pelham, W. (1993). Attention Deficit Hyperactivity Disorder. In R. T. Ammerman & C. G. Last (Eds.), *Handbook of prescriptive*

Treatments for Children and Adolescents (pp. 64-84). Boston: Allyn & Bacon.

Hoza, B., Mrug, S., Gerdes, A.C., Hinshaw, S.P. Bukowski, W.M.L., Gold, J.A., Kraemer, H.C., Pelham, W.E., Wigal, T., & Arnold, L.E. (2005). What Aspects of Peer Relationships are Impaired in Children with Attention-deficit/Hyperactivity Disorder. *Journal of Consulting and Clinical Psychology*, 73, 411-423.

Hynd, G. W., Semrud-Clikeman, M., & Lorys, A. R. (1991). Corpus Callosum Morphology in Attention-Deficit Hyperactivity Disorder (ADHD) : Morphometric Analysis of MRI. *Journal of Learning Disabilities*, 24, 141-146.

Hynd, G.W., Hern, K.L., Novey, E.S., Eliopulos, D., Marshall, R., Gonzalez, J.J., et al. (1993). Attention Deficit Hyeractivity Disorder and Assymetry of the Caudate Nucleus. *Journal of Child Neurology*, 8, 339-347.

Hynd, G.W., Lorys, A.R., Semrud-Clikeman, M., Nieves, N., Huettner, M.I.S., & Lahey, B.B. (1991). Attention Deficit Disorder Without Hyperactivity (ADD/WO) : A Distinct Behavioural and Neurocognitive Syndrome. *Journal of Child Neurology*, 6, S37-S43.

Imhof, M. (2004). Effects of Colorus Stimulation on Handwriting Performance of Children with ADHD Without and with Additional Learning Disabilities. *European Child & Adolescent Psychiatry*, 13, 191-198.

Jacobson, A., & Kikas, E. (2007). Cognitive Functioning in Children With and Without Attention-deficit/Hyperactivity Disorder With and Without Comorbid Learning Disabilities. *Journal of Learning Disabilities*, 40, 3, 194-202.

Jarvinen, D.W. & Sprague, R. L. (1995). Using ACT e RS to Screen Minority Children for ADHD : An examination of Item Bias. *Journal of Psycho-educational Assessment*, 13, 172-184.

Javorsky, J. (1996). An Examination of Youth with Attention Deficit/ Hyperactivity Disorder and Language Learning Disabilites : A Clinical Study. *Journal of Learning Disabilities*, 29, 247-258.

Javorsky, J., & Gussin, B. (1994). College Students with Attention Deficit Hyperactivity Disorder : An Overview and Description of Services. *Journal of College Student Development*, 35, 170-177.

Jennings, J., Van der Molen, M., Pelham, W., Brock, K., & Hoza, B. (1997). Psycho-physiology of Inhibition in Boys with Attention Deficit Disorder. *Developmental Psychology*, 33, 308 – 318.

Jensen, P.S. Shervette, R.E., Xenakis, S.N., & Richters, J. (1993). Anxiety and Depressive Disorders in Attention Deficit Disorders with Hyperactivity: New Findings. *American Journal of Psychiatry,* 150, 1203-1209.

Jensen, P.S., Hinshaw, S.P., Kraemer, H.C., Lenora, N., New Corn, J.H., Abikoff, H.B., et al. (2001). ADHD Comorbidity Findings from the MTA Study : Comparing Comorbid Subgroups. *Journal of the American Academy of Child and Adolescent Psychiatry.* 40, 147-158.

Jerome, L., & Segal, A. (1997). ADHD and Dangerous Driving. *Journal of the American Academy of Child and Adolescent Psychiatry,* 36, 13-25.

Jerome, L., Gordon, M., & Hustler, P. (1994). A Comparison of American and Canadian Teachers' Knowledge and Attitudes Towards ADHD. *Canadian Journal of Psychiatry,* 39, 563-567.

Johnson, B. D., Altmaier, E. M., & Richman, L. C. (1999). Attention Deficits and Reading Disabilities : Are Immediate Memory Defects Additive? *Developmental Neuro-psychology,* 15, 213-226.

Jonkman, L.M., Kemner, C., Verbaten, M.N., Van Engeland, H., Kenemans, J. L., Camfferman, G., et al. (1999). Perceptual and Response Interference in Children with Attention-deficit Hyperactivity Disorder, and the Effects of Methyl-phenidate. *Psychophysiology,* 36, 419-429.

Kagan, J. (1966). Reflection-impulsivity : The Generality and Dynamics of Conceptual Tempo. *Journal of Abnormal Psychology,* 59, 354-357.

Kalff, A., De Sonneville, L., Hurks, P., Hendriksen, J., Kroes, M., Feron, F. et al. (2003). Low and High Level Controlled Processing in Executive Motor Control Tasks in 5-6 year Old Children at Risk of ADHD. *Journal of Child Psychology and Psychiatry and Allied Disciplines,* 44, 1049-1057.

Kandel, E., Mednick, S.A., Kirkegaard-Sorensen, L., Hutchings, B., Knop, J., Rosemberg, R., & Schulsinger, F. (1988). IQ as a Protective Factor for Subjects at High Risk for Antisocial Behaviour. *Journal of Consulting and Clinical Psychology,* 56, 224-226.

Kaplan, B.J., Crawford, S. G., Dewey, D.M., Fisher, G.C. (2000). The IQs of Children with ADHD are Normally Distributed. *Journal of Learning Disabilities,* 33, 5, 425-432.

Kelly, M.L. (1990). *School Home Notes : Promoting Children's Classroom Success.* New York : Guilford.

Kendall, P.C. (2000). *Childhood Disorders.* East Sussex Psychology Press Limited, pp. 60-80.

Klein, R. G. (1998, November). *Alcohol. Nicotine, Stimulants, and Other Drugs*. Paper presented at NIH Consensus Development Conference: Diagnosis and Treatment of Attention Deficit Hyperactivity Disorder, Bethesda, MD.

Klein, R. G., & Manuzza, S. (1991). Long-term Outcome of Hyperactive Children. *Journal of the Americal Academy of Child and Adolescent Psychiatry*, 30, 383-387.

Klinberg, T., Fernell, E., Olesen, P.J., Johnson, M., Gusta afsson, P., Dahlstrom, K., et al. (2005). Computerized Training of Working Memory in Children with ADHD on A Randomized Controlled Trial. *Journal of the American Academy of Child and Adolescent Psychiatry*, 44, 177-186.

Konold, T.R. & Glutting, J.J. (2008). ADHD and Method Variance : A Latent Variable Approach Applied to a Nationally Representative Sample of College Freshmen. *Journal of Learning Disabilities*, 41, 5, 405-416.

Kooistra, L., Crawford, S., Dewey, D., Cantell, M. C., & Kaplan, B. J. (2005). Motor Correlates of ADHD : Contribution of Reading Disability and Oppositional Defiant Disorder. *Journal of Learning Disabilities*, 38, 3, 195-206.

Kos, J.M., Richdale, A.L., & Jackson, M.S. (2004). Knowledge about Attention Deficit/Hyperactivity Disorder : A Comparison of inservice and Pre-service Teachers. *Psychology in the School*, 41, 517-526.

Kroese, J. M., Hynd, G. W., Knight, D. F., Hiemenz, J. R., & Hall, J. (2000). Clinical Appraisal of Spelling Ability and Its Relationship to Phonemic Awareness (Blending, Segmenting, Elision and Reversal), Phonological Memory and Reading in Reading Disabled, ADHD and Normal Children. *Reading and Writing*, 13, 105-131.

Kuperman, S., Kramer, J., & Loney, J. (1988). Enzyme activity and Behaviour in Hyperactive Children Grown-up. *Biological Psychiatry*, 24, 375-383.

Laasonen, M., Lehtinen, M., Leppamaki, S., Tani, P., & Hokkanen, L. (2010). Project DyADD : Phonological Processing, Reading, Spelling, Arithmetic in Adults with Dyslexia or ADHD. *Journal of Learning Disabilities*, 43, 1, 3-14.

Laasonen, M., Leppamaki, S., Tani, P. & Hokkanen, L. (2009). Adult dyslexia and attention disorder in Finland-Project DyAdd : WAIS-III cognitive profiles. *Journal of Learning Disabilities*, 42, 6, 511-527.

Lahey, B. B., Applegate, B., McBurnett, K., Biederman, J., Greenhill, L., Hynd, G. W. et. al. (1994). DSM-IV Field Trials for Attention Deficit

Hyperactivity Disorder in Children and Adolescents. *American Journal of Psychiatry*, 151, 1673-1685.

Lahey, B. B., Pelham, W. E., Loney, J., Lee, S. S., & Wilcutt, E. (2005). Instability of the DSM-IV Subtypes of ADHD from Pre-school through elementary school. *Archives of General Psychiatry*, 62, 896-902.

Lahey, B. B., Schaughency, E. A., Hynd, G. W., Carlson, C. L., & Nieves, N. (1987). Attention Deficit Disorder With and Without Hyperactivity: Comparison of Behavioural Characteristics of Clinic-referred Children. *Journal of the American Academy of Child and Adolescent Psychiatry*, 26, 718-723.

Lahey, B.B., McBurnett, K., & Loeber, R. (2000). Are Attention-deficit Hyperactivity Disorder and Oppositional Defiant Disorder Development Precursors to Conduct Disorder? In M. Lewis & A. Sameroff (Eds.) *Handbook of Developmental Psycho-pathology*. (pp. 431-446). New York : Plenum.

Lahey, B.B., Pelham, W.E., Schaughency, E. A., Atkins, M. S., Murphy, A., Hynd, G., Russo, M., Hartdagen, S., & Lorys-Vernon, A. (1988). Dimensions and Types of Attention Deficit Disorder. *American Journal of Psychiatry*, 27, 330-335.

Lahey, B.B., Pelham, W.E., Stein, M.A., Loney, J., Trapani, C., Nugent, K. *et al.* (1998). Validity of DSM-IV Attention Deficit/ Hyperactivity Disorder for Younger Children. *Journal of the American Academy of Child and Adolescent Psychiatry*, 37, 695-702.

Lahey, B.B., Schaughency, E.A., Strauss, C.C., & Frame, C.L. (1984). Are Attention Deficit Disorders With and Without Hyperactivity Similar or Dissimilar Disorders? *Journal of the American Academy of Child and Adolescent Psychiatry*, 23, 302-310.

Lambert, N.M. & Hartsough, C.S. (1998). Prospective Study of Tobacco Smoking and Substance Dependencies Among Samples of ADHD and non-ADHD Participants. *Journal of Learning Disabilities*, 31, 6, 533-544.

Lamminmaki, T., Ahonen, T., Narhi, V., Lyytinen, H.& DeBarra, H. (1995). Attention Deficit Hyperactivity Disorder : Are There Differences in Academic Problems ? *Development Neuro-psychology*, 11, 297-310.

Lattoste, G.J., Swanson, J.M., Wigal, S.B., Globe, C., Wigal, T., King, N., et al., (1996). Dopamine D4 Receptor Gene Polymorphism is Associated with Attention Deficit Hyperactivity Disorder. *Molecular Psychiatry*, 1, 121-124.

Lee, D.H., Oakland, T., Jackson, G. & Glutting, J. (2008). Estimated Prevalence of Attention-Deficit/Hyperactivity Disorder Symptoms Among College Freshmen : Gender, Race, and Rater Effects. *Journal of Learning Disabilities*, 41, 4, 371-384.

Lienemann, T.O., & Reid, R. (2008). Using Self-regulated Strategy Development to Improve Expository Writing with Students with Attention Deficit Hyperactivity Disorders. *Exceptional Children*, 74, 4, 471-486.

Lienemann, T.O., Graham, S., Leader-Janssen, E., & Reid, R. (2006). Improving the Writing Performance of Struggling Writers in Second Grade. *Journal of Special Education*, 40, 66-78.

Loeber, R., Brinthaupt, V. P., & Green, S. M. (1990). Attention Deficits, Impulsivity, and Hyperactivity With or Without Conduct Problems : Relationships to Delinquency and Unique Contextual Factors. In R. J. McMohan & R. D. Peters (Eds.), *Behaviour Disorders of Adolescence; Research, Intervention, and Policy in Clinical and School Settings* (pp. 39-61), New York : Plenum Press.

Lorch, E., Milch, R., Sanchez, R., Van den Broek, P., Baer, S., Hooks, K., et al. (2000). Comprehension of Televised Stories in Boys with Attention Deficit/Hyperactivity Disorder and Non-referred Boys. *Journal of Abnormal Psychology*, 109, 321-330.

Lowe, P. & Reynolds. C.R. (2000). Attention Deficit/Hyperactivity Disorder (ADHD). In Cecil C. Reynolds & Elaine Fletcher-Janzen (Eds.), *Encyclopaedia of Special Education*, Second Edition, (Vol.1, pp. 166-173), New York : John Wiley & Sons.

Luk, S. & Leung, P.W. (1989). Conners Teachers' Rating scale; A Validity Study in Hong Kong. *Journal of Child Psychology and Psychiatry*, 30, 785-794.

Manly, T., Robertson, I.H., Anderson, V., & Nimmo-Smith, I. (1999). *TEA-Ch : Test of Everyday Attention for Children : Manual*. Bury St. Edmunds, UK : Thames Valley Test Company.

Mann, J.J., McBride, P.A., Brown, R.P., Linnoila, M., Leon, A.C., DeMeo, M., Mieczkowski, T., Myers, J.E., & Stanley, M. (1992). Relationship Between Central and Peripheral Serotonin Indexes in Depressed and Suicidal Psychiatric patients. *Archives of General Psychiatry*, 49, 442-446.

Mannuzza, S., & Klein, R. G. (2000). Long-term Prognosis in Attention–Deficit/Hyperactivity Disorder. *Child and Adolescent Psychiatric Clinic of North America*, 9, 711-726.

Mannuzza, S., Klien, R. G., Bessler, A., Malloy, P., & LaPadula, M. (1998). Adult Psychiatric Status of Hyperactive Boys Grown up. *American Journal of Psychiatry, 155, 493-498*

Marshall, R. M., Hynd, G. W., Handwerk, M. J., & Hall, J. (1997). Academic Underachievement in ADHD Aubtypes. *Journal of Learning Disabilities,* 30, 635-642.

Martinussen, R., Hayden, J., Hogg. Johnson, S. & Tannock, R. (2005). A Meta-analysis of Working Memory Impairments in Children with Attention-Deficit/Hyperactivity Disorder. *Journal of the American Academy of Child and Adolescent Psychiatry,* 44, 377-384.

Mayes, S.D., Calhoun, S.L. & Crowell, E.W. (2000). Learning Disabilities and ADHD : Overlapping Spectrum Disorders. *Journal of Learning Disabilities,* 33, 417-424.

McGee, R., Partidge, F., Williams, S. & Silva, P. (1991). A Twelve-year Follow-up of pre-school Hyperactivity Children. *Journal of the American Academy of Child and Adolescent Psychiatry,* 17, 37-53.

McGee, R., Williams, S., & Silva, P. (1988). Slow Starters and Long-term Backward Readers: A Replication and Extension. *British Journal of Educational Psychology,* 58 330-337.

McGough, J.J., Smalley, S.L., McCracken, J.T., Yang, M., Del'Homme, M., Lynn, D.E., & Loo, S. (2005). Psychiatric Comorbidity in Adult Attention Deficit Hyperactivity Disorder : Findings from Multiple Families. *American Journal of Psychiatry,* 162, 1621-1627.

McInnes, A., Humphries, T., Hogg. Johnson, S., & Tannock, R. (2003). Listening Comprehension and Working Memory are Impaired in Attention Deficit Hyperactivity Disorder Irrespective of Language Impairement. *Journal of Abnormal Child Psychology,* 8, 640-649.

McLean, J.F., & Hitch, G.J. (1999). Working Memory Impairments in Children with Specific Arithmetic Difficulties. *Journal of Experimental Child Psychology,* 74, 240-260.

McMahon, R.C. (1980). Genetic Etiology in the Hyperactive Child Syndrome: A Critical Review : *American Journal of Orthopsychiatry,* 50, 145-150.

McNamara, J., Vervaeke, Sherri-Leigh, Willoughby, T. (2008). Learning Disabilities and Risk-Taking Behaviour in Adolescents. A Comparison of Those With and Without Comorbid Attention-deficit/ Hyperactivity Disorder. *Journal of Learning Disabilities,* 41, 6, 561-574.

Mealer, C., Morgan, S., & Luscomb, R. (1996). Cognitive Functioning of ADHD and Non-ADHD Boys on the WISC III and WRAML : An Analysis Within a Memory Model. *Journal of Attention disorders*, 1, 133-145.

Mehta, M.A., Goodyear, I.M. & Sahakian, B.J. (2004). Methyl-phenidate Improves Working Memory Function and Set Shifting AD/HD : Relationships to Baseline Memory Capacity. *Journal of Child Psychology and Psychiatry*, 45, 293-305.

Merrell, C., & Tymms, P.B. (2001). Inattention, Hyperactivity, and Impulsiveness : Their Impact on Academic Achievement and Progress. *British Journal of Educational Psychology*, 71, 1, 43-56.

Middleton, F.A. & Strick, P.L. (1994). Anatomical Evidence for Cerebellar and Basal Ganglia Involvement in Higher Cognitive Function. *Science*, 266, 458-461.

Milberger, S., Biederman, J., Faraone, S. V., Chen, L., & Jones, J. (1997). ADHD is Associated with Early Initiation of Cigarette Smoking in Children and Adolescents. *Journal of Academic Child Adolescent Psychiatry*, 36, 37-44.

Milich, R., Loney, J. & Roberts, M. (1986). Playroom Observations of Activity Level and Sustained Attention: Two-year Stability, *Journal of Consulting and Clinical Psychology*, 54, 272-274.

Mirsky, A. F., Anthony, B. J., Duncan, C. C., Dhearn, M.B., & Kellam, S. G. (1991). Analysis of the Elements of Attention : A Neuro-psychological Approach. *Neuro-psychology Review*, 2, 109-145.

Moffitt, T. E. (1990). Juvenile Delinquency and Attention Deficit Disorder: Boys' Developmental Trajectories from Age 3 to Age 15. *Child Development*, 61, 893-910.

Molina, B.S.G. & Pelham, W.E. (2001). Substance Use, Substance Abuse, and LD Among Adolescents with a Childhood History of ADHD. *Journal of Learning Disabilities*, 34, 4, 333-342, 351.

Molina, B., & Pelham, W. E. (1999). Alcohol and Other Substance Use and Abuse in ADHD Adolescents : Patterns of Use Compared to Controls and Prediction from Childhood. In W. E. Pelham (Chair), *Adolescent Substance Use and Abuse : Prediction from Childhood Psycho-pathology and Personality and Mediating Pathways*. Annual Meeting of the American Psychological Association, Boston, August.

Molina, B.S.G. & Pelham, W.E., Jr. (2003). Childhood Predictors of Adolescent Substance Use in a Longitudinal Study of Children with ADHD. *Journal of Abnormal Psychology*, 112, 497-507.

Monuteaux, M.C., Faraone, S.V., Herzig, K., Navsaria, N., & Biederman (2005). ADHD and Dyscalculia : Evidence for Independent Familial Transmission. *Journal of Learning Disabilities*, 38, 1, 86-93.

MTA Co-operative Group (1999). A 14-month Randomized Clinical Trial of Treatment Strategies for Attention Deficit Hyperactivity Disorder (ADHD). *Archives of General Psychiatry*, 56, 1073-1086.

Murphy, K. & Barkley, R. A. (1996). Prevalence of DSM-IV symptoms in Adult Licensed Drivers : Implications for Clinical Diagnosis. *Journal of Attention Disorders*, 1, 147-161.

Murphy, K. R., Barkley, R.A., & Bush, T. (2002). Young Adults with Attention Deficit Hyperactivity Disorder: Subtype Differences in Comorbidity, Educational and Clinical History. *Journal of Nervous and Mental Disease*, 190(3), 147-157.

Murray, C., & Pianta, R. (2007). The Importance of Teacher-student Relationships for Adolescents with High Incidence Disabilities. *Theory into Practice*, 46, 105-112.

National Institute for Health and Clinical Excellence. September 2008. Attention Deficit Hyperactivity Disorders. Diagnosis and Management of ADHD in Children Young People and Adults NICE, Clinical Guideline. No. 72.

Nichols, S. (2000). Parental involvement in Supporting Children with Learning Difficulties. In W. Louden et al., *Mapping the Territory-primary Students with Learning Difficulties : Literacy and Numeracy.* Vol. 1 : Overview (pp. 157-180). Canberra, Australia : Department of Education, Training, and Youth Affairs.

Nigg, J. T., Swanson, J. M., & Hinshaw, S. P. (1997). Covert Visual Spatial Attention in Boys with Attention Deficit Hyperactivity Disorder : Lateral Effects, Methylphenidate Response and Results for Parents. *Neuro-psychologia*, 35, 165-176.

Njiokiktjien, C. (1989). Paediatric Behavioural Neurology. *Clinical Principles*, 1', 254-265.

Norvilitis, J.M., Sun, L., Zhang, J. (2000). ADHD Symptomatology and Adjustment to college in China and the United States. *Journal of Learning Disabilities*, 43, 1, 86-94.

Nussbaum, N., Grant, M., Roman, M., Poole, J., & Bigler, E., (1990). Attention Deficit and the Mediating Effect of Age on Academic and Behavioural Variables. *Journal of Behavioural and Developmental Paediatrics*, 11, 22-26.

O'Leary, K.D. (1980). Pills or Skills for Hyperactive Children. *Journal of Applied Behaviour Analysis,* 13, 191-204.

O'Leary, K.D., Pelham, W.E., Rosenbaum, A. & Price, G.H. (1976). Behavioural Treatment of Hyperkinetic Children : An Experimental Evaluation of Its Usefulness. *Clinical Paediatrics,* 15, 510-515.

Olson, S. (1996). Developmental Perspectives. In S. Sandberg (Ed.), *Hyperactivity Disorders of Childhood* (pp. 149-194). Cambridge, UK : Cambridge University Press.

O'Neill, M.E., & Douglas, V.I. (1991). Study Strategies and Story Recall in Attention Deficit Disorder and Reading Disabilities. *Journal of Abnormal Child Psychology,* 19, 671-692.

Palacios, E.D., & Semrud-Clikeman, M. (2005). Delinquency, Hyperactivity, and Phonological Awareness. A Comparison of Adolescents with ODD and ADHD. *Applied Neuro-psychology,* 12, 94-105.

Parasuraman, R. (2000). The Attentive Brain : Issues and Prospects. In R. Parasuraman (Ed.), *The Attentive Brain* (pp. 3-15). Cambridge, MA: MIT Press.

Pasto, L., & Burack, J. A. (1997). A Developmental Study of Visual Attention 8 Issues of Filtering Efficiency and Focus. *Cognitive Development,* 12, 427-439.

Pennington, B. F., Grossier, D., & Welsh, M. C. (1993). Contrasting Cognitive Deficits in Attention Deficit Hyperactivity Disorder *Versus* Reading Disability. *Developmental Psychology,* 29, 511-523.

Pfiffner, L.J. & Barkley, R.A. (1998). Treatment of ADHD in School Settings. In R.A. Barkley (Ed.) *Attention Deficit Hyperactivity Disorder* (pp. 458 – 490). New York : Guilford.

Philips, A.G. & Carr, G.D. (1987). Cognition and the Basal Ganglia : A Possible Substrate for Procedural Knowledge. *Canadian Journal of Neurological Science,* 14, 381-385.

Pickering, S.J., & Gathercole, S.E. (2001). *Working Memory Test Battery for Children.* London : Harcourt Assessment.

Piek, J. P. , Pitcher, T.M., & Hay, D. A. (1999). Motor Co-ordination and Kinaesthesis in Boys with Attention Deficit-hyperactivity Disorder. *Developmental Medicine and Child Neurology,* 41, 159-165.

Pineda, D.A., Adrila, A., & Rosselli, M. (1999). Prevalence of Attention-deficit/Hyperactivity Disorder Symptoms in 4-to 17-year-old Children in the General Population. *Journal of Abnormal Child Psychology,* 27, 455-462.

Pisecco, S., Baker, D. B., Silva, P. A., & Brooke, M. (2001). Boys with Reading Disabilities and/or ADHD : Distinctions in Early Childhood. *Journal of Learning Disabilities*, 34, 98-106.

Pisecco, S., Wristers, K. & Swank, P. Silva, P.A., & Baker, D.B. (2001). The Effect of Academic Self-concept on ADHD and Anti-social behaviours in Early Adolescence. *Journal of Learning Disabilities*, 34, 5, 450-461.

Pitcher, T. M., Piek, J. P. & Hay, D. A. (2003). Fine and Gross Motor Ability in Males with ADHD. *Developmental Medicine and Child Neurology*, 45, 525-535.

Plomin, R. (1999). Genetics and General Cognitive Ability. *Nature*, 402, C 25-C29.

Posner, M. I., & Raichle, M.E. (1994). *Images of Mind.* New York : Scientific American Books.

Posner, M.I., Inhoff, A.W., Friedrich, E., & Cohen, A. (1987). Isolating Attention Systems : A cognitive-anatomical Analysis. *Psycho-biology*, 15, 107-121.

Preston, A. S., Heaton, S.C., McCann, S.J., Watson, W.D., & Selke, G. (2009). The Role of Multidimensional Attentional Abilities in Academic Skills of Children with ADHD. *Journal of Learning Disabilities*, 42, 3, 240-249.

Purvis, K. L., & Tannock, R. (2000). Phonological Processing, Not Inhibitory Control, Differentiates ADHD and Reading Disability. *Journal of the American Academy of Child and Adolescent Psychiatry*, 39, 485-494.

Purvis, K.L. & Tannock, R. (1997). Language Abilities in Children with Attention Deficit Hyperactivity Disorder, Reading Disabilities, and Normal Controls. *Journal of Abnormal Child Psychology*, 25, 133-144.

Ramirez, C.A., Rosen, L.A., Deffenbacher, J.L., Hurst, H., Nicoletta, C., Rosencranz, T., *et al* (1997). Anger and Anger Expression in Adults with High ADHD Symptoms. *Journal of Attention Disorders*, 2, 115-128.

Rapport, M.D., Carlson, G.A., Kelly, K.L., & Pataki, C. (1993). Methylphenidate and Desipramine in Hospitalized Children : 1.Separate and combined Effects on Cognitive Function. *Journal of the American Academy of Child and Adolescent Psychiatry*, 32, 333-342.

Re, A. M., & Cornoldi, C. (2007, May). A Procedural Facilitation Does Not Necessarily Improve Expressive Writing skills of ADHD Children. Presentation at the National AIDAI Conference, Assisi, Italy.

Re, A. M., Caeran, M., Cornoldi, C. (2008). Improving Expressive Writing Skills of Children-rated for ADHD Symptoms. *Journal of Learning Disabilities*, 41, 6, 535-544.

Re, A.M., Pedron, M., & Cornoldi, C. (2007) : Expressive Writing Difficulties in Children Described as Exhibiting ADHD Symptoms. *Journal of Learning Disabilities*, 40, 3, 244-255.

Reader, M.J., Harris, E.L., Schuerholz, L. J., Denckla, M.B. (1994). Attention-deficit Hyperactivity Disorder and Executive Function. *Developmental Neuro-psychology*, 10, 493-512.

Reid, K., & Valle, J.W. (2004). The Discursive Practice of Learning Disability: Implications for Instruction and Parent School Relation. *Journal of Learning Disabilities*, 37, 6, 466-481.

Reid, R., DuPaul, G.J., Power, T.J., Anastopoulas, A.D., Rogers-Adkinson, D., Noll, M., *et al* (1998). Assessing Culturally Different Students for Attention Deficit Hyperactivity Disorder Using Behaviour rating Scales. *Journal of Abnormal Child Psychology*, 26, 187-198.

Reid, R., Maag, J.W., Vasa, S.F. & Wright, G. (1994). Who Are the Children with Attention Deficit Hyperactivity Disorder? A School Based Survey. *Journal of Special Education*, 28, 117-137.

Reid, R., Trout, A. & Schartz, M. (2005). Self-regulation Interventions for Children with Attention Deficit/Hyperactivity Disorder. *Exceptional Children*, 71, 361-377.

Reilley, S.P. (2005). Empirically Informed Attention Deficit/Hyperactivity Disorder Evaluation of College Students. *Journal of College Counselling*, 8, 153-164.

Resnick, R.J. (2005). Attention Deficit Hyperactivity Disorder in Teens and Adults : They Don't all Outgrow It. *Journal of Clinical Psychology*, 61, 529-533.

Resta, S., & Eliot, J. (1994). Written Expression in Boys with Attention Deficit Disorder. *Perceptual & Motor Skills*, 79, 1131-1138

Reynolds, C.R., & Kamphaus, R.W. (1994). *Behaviour Assessment System* for Children. Circle Pines, MN : American Guidance Service.

Richards, G.P., Samuels, S.J., Turnure, J.E., & Isseldyke, J.E. (1990). Sustained and Selective Attention in Children with Learning Disabilities. *Journal of Learning Disabilities*, 23, 129-136.

Richards, T.L., Deffenbacher, J.L., & Rose/n, L.A. (2002). Driving Anger and Other Driving Related Behaviours in High and Low ADHD Symptom College Students. *Journal of Attention Disorders*, 6, 25-38.

Riley, C., DuPaul, G.J., Pipan, M., Kern, L., Brakle, J.V., & Blum, N.J. (2008). Combined Type *versus* ADHD Predominantly Hyperactive Impulsive Type : Is there a Difference in Functional Impairment? *Journal of Developmental and Behavioural Peadiatrics*, 29, 4, 270-275.

Roodenrys, S. (2006). Working Memory Function in Attention Deficit Hyperactivity Disorder. In T.P. Alloway & S.E. Gathercole (Eds.), *Working Memory and Neuro-developmental Disorders* (pp. 187-212). Hove, UK: Psychology Press.

Rosenberg, M.S. (1996). Current Issues Facing Teacher Education and Special Education. *Teacher Education and Special Education*, 19, 209-210.

Ross, P.A., Poidevant, J.M., & Miner, C.U. (1995). Curriculum-based Assessment of Writing Fluency in Children with Attention Deficit Hyperactivity Disorder and Normal Children. *Reading and Writing Quarterly : Overcoming Learning Difficulties*, 11, 201-208.

Rosvold, H.E., Mirsky, A.F., Sarason, I., Bransome, E.D., & Beck, L.H. (1956). A Continuous Performance Test of Brain Damage. *Journal of Consulting Psychology*, 20, 343-352.

Rutter, M. (1977). Brain Damage Syndromes in Childhood : Concepts and Findings. *Journal of Child Psychology and Psychiatry*, 139, 21-33.

Samuelsson, S., Lundberg, I., & Herkner, B. (2004). ADHD and Reading Disability in Male Adults : Is There a Connection ? *Journal of Learning Disabilities*, 37, 2, 155-168.

Sandberg, S., Day, R., & Trott, G.E. (1996). Clinical Aspects. In S. Sandberg (Ed.), *Hyperactivity Disorders of Childhood* (pp. 69-110). Cambridge, UK: Cambridge University Press.

Sandson, T.A., Bachna, K. J., & Morin, M.D. (2000). Right Hemisphee dysfunction in ADHD . Visual Hemispatial Inattention and Clinical Subtype. *Journal of Learning Disabilities*, 33, 83-88.

Scahill, L. & Schwab-Stone, M. (2000). Epidemiology of ADHD in School-Age Children. *Child and Adolescent Psychiatric Clinics of North America*, 9, 541-555.

Schachar, R. J. & Logan, G. D. (1990). Impulsivity and Inhibitory Control in Normal Development and Childhood Psycho-pathology. *Development Psychology*, 26, 710-720.

Schuck, S.E.B., & Crinella, F. M. (2005). Why Children with ADHD Do Not Have Low IQs. *Journal of Learning Disabilities*, 38, 3, 262-280.

Schultz, W. (1998). Predictive Reward Signal of Dopamine Neurons. *Journal of Neuro-physiology*, 80, 1-27.

Schwean, V.L., Saklofske, D.H., Yackulic, R.A. & Quinn, D. (1993) . WISC-III Performance of ADHD Children. *Journal of Psycho-educational Assessment. Monograph Series : Advances in Psycho-educational Assessment*, 56-70.

Sciutto, M.J., Terjesen, M.D., & BenderFrank, A.S. (2000). Teachers' Knowledge and Misperceptions of Attention Deficit Hyperactivity Disorder. *Psychology in the Schools*, 37, 115-22.

Seguin, J. R., Pihl, R.O., Harden, P.W., Tremblay, R.E., & Boulerice, B. (1995). Cognitive and Neuro-psychological Characteristics of Physically aggressive boys. *Journal of Abnormal Psychology*, 104, 614-624.

Seidman, L. (1997). Neuro-psychological Testing. In A. Tasman, J. Kay, & J. Liberman (Eds.), *Psychiatry* (pp. 498-508). Philadelphia : Saunders.

Seidman, L. J., Biederman, J., Faraone, S. V., Weber, W., & Ouellette, C. (1997). Toward Defining a Neuro-psychology of Attention Deficit-hyperactivity Disorder. Performance of Children and Adolescents from a Large Clinically Referred Sample. *Journal of Consulting and Clinical Psychology*, 65, 150-160.

Seidman, L.J., Biederman, J., Monuteaux, M.C., Doyle, A.E., & Faraone, S.V (2001). Learning Disabilities and Executive Dysfunction in Boys with Attention Deficit Hyperactivity Disorder. *Neuropsychology*, 15, 544-556.

Seidman, L.J., Biederman, J., Weber, W., Hatch, M., & Faraone, S.V. (1998). Neuro-psychological Function in Adults with Attention-deficit Hyperactivity Disorder. *Biological Psychiotry*, 44, 260-268.

Semrud-Clikeman, M.S., Biederman, J., Spirich, S., Buckminster, S., Lehman, B., Norman, D., & Faraone, S. (1992). Comorbidity Between ADDH and Learning Disability : A Review and Report in a Clinically Referred Sample. *Journal of the American Academy of Child and Adolescent Psychiatry*, 31, 439-448.

Sergeant, J. A. & van der Meere, J. J. (1990). Additive Factor Method Applied to Psychopathology with Special Reference to Childhood Hyperactivity. *Acta Psychologica*, 74, 277-296.

Shalev, L., & Tsal, Y. (2003). The Wide Attentional Window : A Major Deficit of Children with Attentional Difficulties. *Journal of Learning Disabilities*, 36, 517-527.

Shanahan, M.A., Pennington, B.F., Yerys, B.E., Scott, A., Boada, R., Willcutt, E.G. et al., (2006). Processing Speed Deficits in Attention Deficit/ Hyperactivity Disorder and Reading Disability. *Journal of Abnormal Child Psychology*, 34, 585-602.

Shaywitz, B., Fletcher, J., Holahan, J., Sadler, A., Marchione, K., Stuebing, K., et al. (1995). Cognitive Profiles of Reading Disability : Interrelationships Between Reading Disability and Attention Deficit Hyperactivity Disorder. *Child Neuropsychology,* 1, 170-186.

Shin, M., Kim, Y., Cho, S., & Kim B. (2003). Neuro-psychological Characteristics of Children with Attention-Deficit Hyperactive Disorder (ADHD), Learning Disorder, and tic Disorder on the Rey-Osterreith Complex Figure. *Journal of Child Neurology,* 18, 835-844.

Skinner, B.F. (1953). *Science and human behaviour*. New York : Macmillan.

Snider, V.E., Busch, T., & Arrowood, L. (2003). Teacher Knowledge of Stimulant Medication and ADHD. *Remedial and Special Education,* 24, 46-56.

Spafford, C.S. & Grosser, G.S. (1993). The Social Misperception Syndrome in Children with Learning Disabilities : Social Causes *versus* Neurological Variables. *Journal of Learning Disabilities,* 26, 178-198.

Sparks, R.L., Javorsky, J., & Philips, L. (2004). College Students Classified with ADHD and the Foreign Language Requirement. *Journal of Learning Disabilities,* 37, 2, 169-178.

Spencer, T., Biederman, J., Wilen, T., Harding, M., O'Donnell, D. & Griffin, S. (1996). Pharmacotherapy of Attention-Deficit Hyperactivity Disorder Across the Life Cycle. *Journal of the American Academy of Child and Adolescent Psychiatry,* 35, 409-432.

Spencer, T., Biederman, J., Wilens, T. & Faraone, S. (1994). Is Attention Deficit Hyperactivity Disorder in Adults a Valid Disorder ? *Harvard Review of Psychiatry,* 1, 326-335.

Spivak, B., Ioran, R., BarIosef, H., Peres, C., Mester, R., Mozes, T., Blumensohn, R., & Weizman, A. (1997). The Role of Intelligence and Hyperactivity in Diagnosis of Attention Deficit Disorder in Children and Adolescents. *International Journal of Adolescent Medicine and Health, 9,*165-171.

Stanford, L.D., & Hynd, G.W. (1994). Congruence of Behavioural Symptomatology in Children with ADD/H, ADD/WO, and Learning Disabilities, *Journal of Learning Disabilities,* 27, 243-253.

Stanovich, K.E. & Siegel, L.S. (1994). Phenotypic Performance Profile of Children with Reading Disabilities : A Regression-based Test of the phonological Core Variable Difference Model. *Journal of Educational Psychology,* 86, 24-53.

Steger, J., Imhof, K., Coutts, E., Gundelfinger, R., Steinhausen, H. –C., & Brandeis, D. (2001). Attentional and Neuromotor Deficits in ADHD. *Developmental Medicine and Child Neurology*, 43, 172-179.

Sternberg, R. J. (1984). Toward a Triarchic Theory of Human Intelligence. *Behaviour and brain sciences*, 2, 269-315.

Sternberg, R. J. (1985). *Beyond I Q : A Triarchic Theory of Human Intelligence.* New York : Cambridge University Press.

Stevenson, J., Pennington, B.F., Gilger, J.W., DeFries, J.C., & Gillis, J. J. (1993). Hyperactivity and Spelling Disability : Testing for Shared Genetic Aetiology. *Journal of Child Psychology and Psychiatry*, 14, 1137-1152.

Still, G.F. (1902). Some Abnormal Psychical Conditions in Children. The Goulstonian Lectures. *Lancet*, 1 : 1008 – 1-12.

Strauss, A.A., & Lehtinen, L.E. (1947). *Psychopathology and Education of the Brain Injured Child.* New York : Grune & Stone.

Strecker, E., & Ebaugh, F. (1924). Neuropsychiatric Sequelae of Cerebral Trauma in Children. *Archives of Neurology and Psychiatry*, 12, 443-453.

Stroop, J. (1935). Studies of Interference in Serial Verbal Reaction. *Journal of Experimental Psychology*, 18, 643-662.

Swanson, H.L. & Sachse-Lee, C. (2001). Mathematical Problem Solving and Working Memory in Children with Learning Disabilities : Both Executive and Phonological Processes are Important. *Journal of Experimental Child Psychology*, 79, 294-321.

Swanson, H.L., Zheng, X., & Jerman, O. (2009). Working Memory, Short-Term Memory and Reading Disabilities : A Selective Meta-analysis of the Literature. *Journal of Learning Disabilities*, 42, 3, 260-287.

Swanson, J., & Kinsbourne, M. (1980). Artificial Color and Hyperactive Children. In R.M. Knights & D.J. Bakker (Eds.), *Treatment of Hyperactive and Learning Disabled Children.* Baltimore : University Park Press.

Swanson, J., Oosterlaan, J., Murias, M., Schuck, S., Flodman, P., Spence, M.A., et al. (2000). Attention Deficit/Hyperactivity Disorder Children with a 7 Repeat Allele of the Dopamine Receptor D4 Gene have Extreme Behavior but Normal Performance on Critical Neuro-psychological Tests of Attention. Proceedings of the National Academy of Sciences of the United states of America, 97, 4754-4759.

Swanson, J., Posner, M. I., Cantwell, D., Wigal, S., Crinella, F., Filipek, P., et al. (2000). Attention Deficit/Hyperactivity Disorder : Symptom

Domains, Cognitive Processes and Neural Networks. In R. Parasuraman (Ed.), *The Attentive Brain* (pp. 445-460). Cambridge, MA: MIT Press.

Swanson, J.M., Sunohara, G.A., Kennedy, J.L. Regino, R., Fineberg, E., Wigal, R., et al. (1998). Association of the Dopamine Receptor D4 (DRD4) Gene with a Refined Phenotype of Attention Deficit Hyperactivity Disorder (ADHD): A Family-based Approach. *Molecular Psychiatry*, 3, 38-41.

Szatsmari, P., Offord. D.R., & Boyle, M.H. (1989). Correlates, Associated Impairments, and Patterns of Service Utilization of Children with Attention Deficit Disorders : Findings from the Ontario Child Health Study. *Journal of Child Psychology and Psychiatry*, 30, 205-217.

Tannock, R. & Schachar, R. (1996). Executive dysfunction as an underlying mechanism of behaviour and language problems in attention deficit hyperactivity disorder. In J.H. Beitchman, N. Cohen, M.M. Konstantareas, & R. Tannock (Eds.), *Language, learning, and behaviour disorders : Developmental, biological and clinical perspectives* (pp. 128 – 155). New York : Cambridge University Press.

Tannock, R. (2000). Attention deficit Disorders with Anxiety Disorders. In T.E. Brown (Ed.), *Attention Deficit Disorders and Comorbidities in Children, Adolescents, and Adults* (pp. 125-170). Washington, DC: American Psychiatric Press.

Taranowski, K. J., Prinz, R. J., & Nay, S. M. (1986). Comparative Analysis of Attentional Deficits in Hyperactive and Learning Disabled Children. *Journal of Abnormal Psychology*, 95, 341-345.

Taylor, E. (1994). Syndromes of Attention Deficit and Overactivity. In M.Rutter, E. Taylor, & L. Hersov (Eds.), *Child and Adolescent Psychiatry* (pp. 285-307). Oxford UK : Blackwell Scientific Publications.

Thompson, R. (1982a). Brain Lesions Impairing Visual and Spatial Reversal Learning in Rats : Components of the "General Learning System" of the Rodent Brain. *Physiological Psychology*, 10, 186-198.

Thompson, R. (1982b). Impaired Visual and Spatial Reversal Learning in Brain Damaged Rats : Additional Components of the "General Learning System" of the Rodent Brain. *Physiological Psychology*, 10, 293-305.

Thompson, R., & Yang, S. (1982). Retention of Individual Spatial Reversal Problems in Rats with Nigral, Caudatoputamenal, and Reticular Formation Lesions. *Behavioral and Neural Biology*, 34, 98-103.

Thompson, R., Bjelajac, V.M., Fukui, S., Huestis, P.W., Crinella, F.M. & Yu, J. (1989). Failure to Transfer Digging Response to a Detour Problem in Young Rats with Lesions to the "General Learning system". *Physiology and Behavior*, 45, 1235-1241.

Thompson, R., Bjelajac, V.M., Huestis, P.W., Crinella, F.M., & Yu, J. (1989). Inhibitory Deficits in Rats Rendered "Mentally Retarded" by Early Brain Damage. *Psychobiology*, 17, 61-76.

Thompson, R., Crinella, F.M., & Yu, J. (1990). *Brain Mechanisms in Problem Solving and Intelligence : A Lesion Survey of the Rat Brain*. New York : Plenum Press.

Thompson, R., Harmon, D., & Yu, J. (1984). Detour Problem Solving Behaviour in Rats with Neocortical and Hippocampal Lesions : A Study of Response Flexibility. *Physiological Psychology*, 12, 116-124.

Thompson, R., Huestis, P.W., Bjelajac, V.M., Crinella, F.M. & Yu, J. (1989). Working Memory in Young Rats with Lesions to the "General Learning System". *Psychobiology*, 17, 285-292.

Treisman, A.M., & Gelade, G. A. (1980). Feature-Integration Theory of Attention. *Cognitive Psychology*, 12, 97-136.

Tressoldi, P. E. & Cornoldi, C. (1991). *Batteria per la valutazione della scritturae della competenza ortografica nella scuola dell'obbligo* [Battery for the Assessment of Writing Skills of Children from 7 to 13 years old]. Florence, Italy : Organizzazioni speciali.

Treuting, J.J., & Hinshaw, S.P. (2001). Depression and self-esteem in Boys with Attention-Deficit/Hyperactivity Disorder : Associations with Comorbid Aggression and Explanatory Attributional Mechanisms, *Journal of Abnormal Child Psychology*, 29, 23-39.

Tsal, Y., Shalev, L., & Mevorach, C. (2005). The Diversity of Attention Deficits in ADHD : The Prevalence of Four Cognitive Factors in ADHD *versus* Controls. *Journal of Learning Disabilities*, 38, 2, 142-157.

Tucha, O. & Lange, K. W. (2004). Handwriting And Attention in Children and Adults with Attention Deficit Hyperactivity Disorder. *Motor Control*, 8, 461-471.

Unsworth, N., & Engle, R.W. (2007). On the Division of Short-term Memory and Working Memory : An Examination of Simple and Complex Span and Their Relation to Higher Order Abilities. *Psychological Bulletin*, 133, 1038-1066.

Van der Meere, J. (1996). The Role of Attention In S. Sandberg (Ed.), *Hyperactivity Disorders of Childhood* (pp. 111-148). Cambridge, UK: Cambridge University Press.

Van Kraayenoord, C.E., & Elkins, J. (2004). Learning Difficulties in Numeracy in Australia. *Journal of Learning Disabiltiies,* 37, 1, 32-41.

Van Luit, J.E.H., Kroesbergen, E.H., & Naglieri, J. A. (2005). Utility of the PASS Theory and Cognitive Assessment System for Dutch Children With and Without ADHD. *Journal of Learning Disabilities,* 38, 5, 434-439.

Van Mourik, R., Oosterlaan, J. & Sergeant, J.A. (2005). The Stroop Revisited: A Meta-analysis of Interference Control in AD/HD. *Journal of Child Psychology & Psychiatry,* 46, 150-165.

Wahler, R.G., & Dumas, J.E. (1989). Attentional Problems in Dysfunctional Mother-child Interactions. *Psychological Bulletin,* 105, 116-130.

Warner-Rogers, J., Taylor, A., Taylor, E., & Sandberg, S. (2000). Inattentive Behaviour in Childhood : Epidemiology and Implications for Development. *Journal of Learning Disabilities,* 33, 6, 520-536.

Wechsler, D. (2001). *Wechsler Individual Achievement Test-Second Edition (WIAT-II),* San Antonio, TX : Psychological Corporation.

Weiss, G. & Hechtman, L. (1986) *Hyperactive Children Grownup.* New York : Guilford Press.

Weiss, G. & Hechtman, L. (1993). *Hyperactive Children grown up* (2nd ed.) New York : Guilford.

Weiss, G., Hetchman, L., Milroy, T., & Perlman, T. (1985). Psychiatric Status of Hyperactives as Adults : A Controlled Prospective 15 year Follow-up of 63 Hyperactive Children. *Journal of the Americal Academy of Child and Adolescent Psychiatry,* 24, 211-220.

Welsh, M.C. & Pennington, B. F. (1988). Assessing Frontal Lobe Functioning in Children : Views from Developmental Psychology. *Developmental Neuro-psychology,* 4, 199-230.

Wender, P.H (2002). ADHD: *Attention Deficit Hyperactivity Disorder in Children and Adults.* Oxford University Press, 2002 (p.9).

West, J., Taylor, M., Houghton, S., & Hudyma (2005). A Comparison of Teachers' and Parents Knowledge and Beliefs About ADHD. *School Psychology International,* 26, 192-208.

Weyandt, L.L., Iwaszuk, W., Fulton, K., Ollerton, M., Beatty, N., Fouts, H., et al. (2003). The Internal Restlessness Scale : Performance of College Students With and Without ADHD. *Journal of Learning Disabilities,* 36, 382-389.

Whalen, C. K., & Henker, B. (1991a). Social Impact of Stimulant Treatment for Hyperactive Children. *Journal of Learning Disabilities,* 24, 231-241.

Whalen, C.K., & Henker, B. (1991b). Therapies for Hyperactive Children: Comparisons, Combinations, and Compromises. *Journal of Consulting and Clinical Psychology*, 59, 126-137.

Willcutt, E. G., & Pennington, B. F. (2000). Comorbidity of Reading Disabilities and Attention Deficit Hyperactivity Disorder : Differences by Gender and Subtype. *Journal of Learning Disabilities*, 33, 179-191.

Willcutt, E.G., Doyle, A.D., Nigg, J.T., Faraone, S.V., & Pennington, B.F. (2005). Validity of the Executive Function Theory of Attention-Deficit/Hyperactivity Disorder. A Meta-Analytic Review. *Biological Psychiatry*, 57, 1336-1346.

Willcutt, E.G., Pennington, B.F., Boada, R., Ogline, J.S., Tunick, R.A., Chhabildas, N.A., et al. (2001). A Comparison of the Cognitive Deficits in Reading Disability and Attention-deficit/Hyperactivity Disorder. *Journal of Abnormal Psychology*, 110, 157-172.

Willcutt, E.G., Pennington, B.F., Olson, R. K., Chhabildas, N. & Hulslander, J. (2005). Neuropsychological Analyses of Comorbidity Between Reading Disability and Attention Deficit Hyperactivity Disorder : In Search of the Common Deficit. *Developmental Neuropsychology*, 27, 35-78.

Wilson, J. & Marcotte, A.C. (1996). Psychosocial Adjustment and Educational Outcome in Adolescents with a Childhood Diagnosis of Attention Deficit Disorder. *Journal of the American Academy of Child and Adolescent Psychiatry*, 35, 5, 579-587.

Wolf, L.E. (2001). College Students with ADHD and Other Hidden Disabilities : Outcomes and Interventions. In J. Wasserstein, & L.E. Wolf (Eds.), *Adult Attention Deficit Disorder Brain Mechanisms and Life Outcomes*. (pp. 385-395). New York : New York Academy of Scineces.

Wolraich, M., Milich, R., Stumbo, P., & Schultz, F. (1985). The Effects of Sucrose Ingestion on the Behaviour of Hyperactive Boys. *Pediatrics*, 106, 657-682.

Wolraich, M.L., Hannah, J.N., Pinnock, T.Y., Baumgaertel, A., & Brown, J. (1996). Comparison of Diagnostic Criteria for Attention Deficit Hyperactivity in a Country-wide Sample. *Journal of the American Academy of Child and Adolescent Psychiatry*, 35, 319 – 324.

Woods, S.P., Lovejoy, D.W., & Ball, J.D. (2002). Neuro-psychological Characteristics of Adults with ADHD : A Comprehensive Review of Initial Studies. *Clinical Neuro-psychologist*, 16, 12-34.

World Health Organization (1977). *Manual of the International Statistical Classifiction of Diseases Injuries, and Causes of Death* (9th revision) Geneva, Switzerland : Author.

World Health Organization (1978). *Glossary and Guide to Their Classification in Accordance with the Ninth Revision of the International Classification of Diseases.* Geneva, Switzerland : Author.

World Health Organization (1992a). International Statistical Classification of Diseases and Related Health Problems (10th rev.) Geneva, Switzerland : Author.

World Health Organization (1992b). The ICD-10 Classification of Mental and Behavioural Disorders : Clinical Descriptions and Diagnostic Guidelines. Geneva, Switzerland : Author.

World Health Organization (1993). The ICD-10 Classification of Mental and Behavioural Disorders: Diagnostic Criteria for Research. Geneva, Switzerland : Author.

Yang, K. N., Schaller, J. L., & Parker, R. (2000). Factor Structures of Taiwanese Teachers' Ratings of ADHD : A Comparison with U.S. studies. *Journal of Learning Disabilities*, 33, 1, 72-82.

Ysseldyke, J.E., & Algozzine, B. (2006). *Special Education : A Practical Approach for Teachers.* (pp. 432 – 433), New Delhi : Kanishka Publishers.

Zahn-Waxler, C., Duggal, S., & Gruber, R. (2002). Parental Psychopathology. In *Handbook of Parenting*, Vol. 4, 2nd ed., ed. M.H. Bornstein, 295-327. Mahwah, NJ : Lawrence Erlbaum.

Zental, S. (1990). Fact-retrieval Automatization and Math Problem Solving by Learning Disabled, Attention Disordered and Normal Adolescents. *Journal of Educational Psychology*, 82, 856-865.

Zentall, S. & Kruczek, T. (1988). The Attraction of Color for Active Attention-Problem Children. *Exceptional Children*, 54, 357-362.

Zentall, S. (1993). Research on the Educational Implications of Attention Deficit Hyperactivity Disorder. *Exceptional Children*, 60, 143-153.

Zentall, S., Smith, Y., Lee, Y., & Wieczorek, C. (1994). Mathematical Outcomes of Attention-Deficit Hyperactivity Disorder. *Journal of Learning Disabilities*, 27, 510-519.

Zentall, S.S. (2005). *ADHD and education.* Columbus, OH: Pearson.

Glossary

Anxiety : In psychology or medicine, a strong, unrealistic, and sometimes irrational fear, a common characteristic of serious emotional disturbances.

Assessment : Process of collecting data to make decisions about students.

Category : In special education, a grouping of exceptional students who are thought to share certain characteristics. Although professionals attempt to standardize the names and definitions of categories, there is significant variation from one state to another.

Central nervous system : Brain and spinal cord.

Chromosome : Very fine thread like structures inside the nucleus of cell that bear genes.

Communication : The process by which individuals interact to transmit and receive messages by any means, including sounds, symbols, gestures, and others.

Communication disorder : Impairment in speech or language that interferes significantly with a person's ability to communicate.

Comorbidity : Overlap or co-existence of more than one developmental disorder.

Conduct disorder : Persistent and repetitive 'acting-out' behaviour problem in which the rights of others or societal rules are violated; represents a variety of serious anti-social acts such as aggression, destruction of property, deceitfulness or theft, serious violation of rules.

Congenital : Any condition which is present at birth. Contrasts with adventitious handicap.

Cortex : The outer layer of an organ. Usually refers to the outer gray cells of the brain.

Delinquency : Antisocial or illegal behaviour exhibited by a child or adolescent.

Diagnosis : (*i*) Determining the nature of an educational task or problem; see instructional diagnosis; (*ii*)Effort to identify the extent to which a student's poor performance is caused by poor instruction and to determine possible remedies.

Direct Instruction : Instruction in which teacher's actions are directly and functionally related to the goals of instruction; generally emphasizes systematic teaching of specific components of each desired skill.

Disability : Medical, social or learning difficulty that interferes significantly with an individual's normal growth and development.

Disruptiveness : Pattern of behaviours that interfere with educational activities or cause annoyance or disturbance to others in the school.

Dizygotic twins : Twins resulting from the fertilization of two ova by two separate sperm cells. They may be of the same sex or of opposite sexes. Same as fraternal twins.

Early intervention : Educational and other services provided before a child reaches school age or before school related problems become serious.

Education : Process of learning and changing as a result of schooling and other experiences.

Educational Environment : Any setting in which education or training takes place including schools, institutions, training centres, day care centres, group homes, workshops and private homes.

Enrichment : (*i*) Enhancing the educational experience of students with materials or activities that go beyond the standard curriculum; does not involve changing student's placement or educational setting. (*ii*) An educational approach which involves providing a child with extra learning experiences which the standard curriculum would not normally include. Most often used with gifted and talented children.

Etiology : The science of the causes and origin of disease.

Evaluation : The process by which teachers decide whether their methods and materials are affective on the basis of individual student's performance.

Externalizing disorders : Outer directed maladaptive behaviour problem that causes problem to others, e.g., conduct disorder.

Factor analysis : A method for determining the number and nature of the underlying variables among large number of measures.

Feedback : Information provided to students about their performance.

Hearing impairment ; A hearing problem that adversely affects a student's educational performance.

Hyper : Prefix meaning 'increased', 'over' or 'excessive'. Opposite of hypo.

Hyper-active behaviour : Excessive motor activity or restlessness.

Identical twins : Twins resulting from the fertilization of a single ovum by a single sperm cell. The cell subsequently divides to form two identical individuals who are always of the same sex. Synonymous with monozygotic twins.

Incidence : The percentage of people who, at some time in their lives, will be identified as having a specific handicapping condition.

Inclusion : Educating exceptional students regardless of type or severity of disability in regular class-rooms in their neighbourhood schools. Also known as full inclusion.

Internalizing disorder : Behaviour problem that is inner directed, e.g., anxiety, depression.

Intervention : All the effort made on behalf of the handicapped may be preventive, remedial or compensatory.

Interviewing : Arising questions to obtain information about an individual's background, current levels of performance, and plans.

Label : Generally, a verbal cue that helps organize knowledge, perceptions, and behaviour. In special education labels are names assigned to behaviours, people or the conditions people exhibit.

Language disorder : Impairment that affects use of proper forms of language (phonology, morphology or syntax), the content of language (semantics) or the functions of language (pragmatics).

Learning disability : Disorder in one or more the basic psychological process involved in understanding or using language; may manifest itself in an imperfect ability to listen, think, speak, read, write, spell, or do mathematical calculations. Often identified by discrepancy between expected and actual achievement. Also called specific learning disability.

Mobility : Ability to more safely and efficiently from one place to another or from one point to another.

Monozygotic twins : Same as identical twins.

Non-attention : Not paying attention to the task at hand.

Observing : Watching an individual perform a set of behaviours to obtain information about the rate or duration of those behaviours.

Oppositional behaviour : Not doing what some-one else (such as the teacher) has requested also called non-compliance.

Outcomes : Specific results of the educational process; what students know and are able to do as a result of their schooling experiences.

Peer-tutoring : Students' teaching class-mates or peers with teacher supervision.

Phenylketonuria (PKU) : An inherited metabolic disease which can cause severe retardation; can now be detected at birth and the detrimental effects prevented with special diet.

Phonological awareness : It refers to the awareness of the sound structure of spoken language.

Phonological memory : It refers to the coding and temporary storage of sound-based representations.

Phonological naming : It refers to the rapid access of phonological information stored in long-term memory.

Phonological processing : It refers to processing of the phonological or sound structure of oral and written language. According to one view it comprises of three subprocess phonological awareness, phonological memory, and phonological naming. According to another view phonological awareness and phonological naming are independent processes.

Physical disability : Impairment in movement, mobility, neuro-muscular operation or another mode of physical functioning; the term includes conditions in the federal categories of orthopaedic impairment traumatic brain injury and autism.

Positive reinforcement : Any stimulus or event which occurs after a behaviour has been emitted that has the effect of increasing the occurrence of that behaviour in the future.

Prevalence : The number of people who have a certain handicapping condition at any given time.

Programmed learning : Instructional method that involves diagnosing students by pre-established instruments and programming them into sequenced learning resources when they demonstrate content mastery.

Reinforcement : An event, object or statement that increases the frequency of a behaviour.

Remediation : Instruction designed to repair or correct deficit in performance by training students in deficient areas.

Screening : (1) Collecting data to determine whether more intensive assessment is necessary. (2) A procedure where groups of children are examined and/or tested in an effort to identify 'high-risk' children; identified children are then referred for more intensive examination and evaluation.

Serious disability : Disability requiring extensive, continued assistance in more than one major life activity.

Serious emotional disturbance : Condition in which a student exhibits one or more of the following characteristics over a long period and to a marked degree, adversely affecting educational performance; an inability to learn that cannot be explained by intellectual, sensory or health factors, inability to build or maintain satisfactory interpersonal relationships with peers and teachers, inappropriate behaviours or feelings under normal circumstances; a general pervasive mood of unhappiness or depression, or a tendency to develop physical systems or fears associated with personal or school problems. Also called behaviour disorder.

Speech or language impairment : Impairment in speech or language that interferes significantly with a person's ability to communicate.

Substance : Usually refers to nicotine products, alcohol, and illicit drugs.

Substance abuse : Refers to substance dependence to the extent of meeting clinical criteria for a disorder.

Substance use : Indicates levels of substance use that although illegal and risky, do not meet clinical criteria for a disorder.

Testing : Administering a set of items to obtain a score.

Time out : A behaviour management technique which involves removing the opportunity for the child to be reinforced for a specific period of time following an inappropriate behaviour; results in a reduction of inappropriate behaviour.

Index